JEWISH ARCHITECTURE
By Gary Berkovich

Berkovich, Gary
Jewish Architecture

Copyright © 2024 by Gary Berkovich
All rights reserved

No part of this book may be reproduced in any form or by any means, electronic, mechanical, photocopying, or otherwise, without the prior written permission of the author, except for the use of brief quotations in a book review.

Book interior and cover design by Gary Berkovich

ISBN 978-1-68082-056-0
Published in the United States by ALMAZ
10 9 8 7 6 5 4 3 2 1
First Edition

In memory of Marina and Slava Berkovich

Acknowledgments

I would like to express my gratitude to those who helped me develop this book.

First and foremost, I extend my deepest thanks to my son-in-law, Hemmant Jha, whose skepticism about my ideas and the validity of my arguments regarding Jewish architecture inspired me to write this book. I am also grateful to my daughter, Lana, who, despite rejecting my overall concept of Jewish architecture, helped me refine some of my arguments.

My thanks go as well to my grandson, Jaime, who did his best to find time to read the book and provide feedback. I am especially indebted to my neighbor and friend, Mary Daniels, the first reader of this book, for her time, effort, and numerous suggestions for improving the text.

Finally, I am profoundly grateful to my wife, Elena Yordanova, for her unwavering support and tireless efforts in creating the most comfortable working environment for me.

To the Reader

At the outset of my architectural practice in the USA, I once presented the initial sketches of a single-family house to a client who, as it turned out, was a descendant of Irish immigrants. To my surprise, his immediate response was, "Do I look like a Jew? Why are you bringing me Jewish Architecture?" Puzzled, I took a moment to reflect. The house I had envisioned for him boasted an open floor plan and modern shapes. Why, then, does he call it Jewish Architecture?

Lately, intrigued by his observation, and motivated by curiosity, I dedicated myself to a thorough investigation. I set out on a journey of exploration to understand why, not only my client, but many lay people worldwide use the term 'Jewish Architecture' to characterize modern architecture.

It took me several years to comprehend that my Irish client's observation was entirely valid. This book is the culmination of the surprising results I uncovered in my research.

Contents

Acknowledgments	3
To the Reader	5
Introduction	9
Chapter 1. The Jews and the Subject of Architecture	11
Chapter 2. Function, Style, and Epoch in Architecture	21
Chapter 3. National Architecture	43
Chapter 4. Jewish Structures in the Host Countries	71
Chapter 5. Precursors of Global Architecture	91
Chapter 6. *Jewish Architecture*	163
Summary	191
Bibliography	195
Index	199

Introduction

National architecture—whether Chinese, Arabic, French, German, English or any other—encompasses all the buildings within the territory inhabited by the respective people. This architecture mirrors the national character of the nation, the environmental conditions and local materials, as well as construction technologies and practices. The nationality, faith, or social status of the client or architect of each structure holds no significance in this broader context. The Jews did not have the opportunity to cultivate a national architecture compa-rable to that of other nations for they lacked a sovereign territory. They have resided in foreign lands for the past 18 centuries, experienced diverse climate conditions, and employed in their build-ings various local construction materials and methods.

The analysis conducted in this study confirms that the emancipation of the Jews, which coincided with the onset of the Industrial Revolution in the nineteenth century, marked a significant shift in the trajectory of world architecture. It was a pivotal moment within Western civilization, representing a departure from previous architectural paradigms. Whereas since the Renaissance, the architecture paradigm in Western society was rooted in the concept of architecture as a component of art and had been primarily concerned with the embellishment of buildings, but now architecture was increasingly understood as the creation of a habitat. Simultaneously, new art movements such as Arts and Crafts and Art Nouveau along with others emerged in Europe, inspiring new architectural forms. These developments culminated in the modern architecture of the twentieth century, characterized by functionality, open-plan designs, nov-el materials and construction methods, and fresh aesthetic perspectives. Moreover, these architectural transformations happened alongside profound social changes, including globalization, which reshaped the world. This global shift led to the internationalization of architecture, resulting in the emergence of a global architecture with a new language that transcended national boundaries.

The central theme of the book is the genesis of this architecture, shedding light on the pivotal role of Jews in the transformative events of the nineteenth and twentieth centuries.

Before delving into this subject, we need to have a clear understanding of key terms related to various aspects of architecture. The first task is to define the subject of architecture, as well as the concepts of style and fashion within it. In architecture, style and fashion are related solely to its sculptural aspects. However, within academic discourse, style and fashion are frequently applied to architecture as a whole.

The next objective is to investigate whether architectural endeavors undertaken by Jewish communities across different nations can be categorized as Jewish Architecture. This examination involves assessing the distinct characteristics and influences that may define such architecture.

Moreover, it is crucial to analyze the role of Jewish individuals and communi-ties in shaping the architectural para-digms of the nineteenth and twentieth centuries. This exploration delves into the contributions, influences, and innovations brought forth by Jewish clients and financiers, architects, designers, and thinkers, and their impact on the evolution of architectural theory and practice during these transformative periods.

In academic and enlightened circles, the concept of Jewish Architecture deviates from the conventional definition of national architecture, which typically pertains to buildings within a specific nation's territory. Instead, Jewish Architecture in most of the scholarly publications encompasses structures intended for or constructed by Jewish individuals, as well as those buildings infused with a distinct 'Jewish flavor.' This study endeavors to reassess and provide a comprehensive understanding of this notion within its proper context.

The analysis presented in this book aims to demonstrate that despite the Jewish diaspora not constituting a conventional nation for nearly 2,000 years, but during the last 200 years has nonetheless fostered a unique form of international architecture—*Jewish Architecture*. The primary focus of this research is to explore how the Jewish diaspora has played a significant role in shaping and defining this architecture, elucidating its distinctive features.

Chapter 1. The Jews and the Subject of Architecture

To determine if the Jews as a nation created their architecture, it is crucial to recognize whether the Jews of the worldwide diaspora constitute a nation. It is a subject of ongoing debate with multifaceted interpretations, incorporating historical, cultural, religious, and political perspectives. Several arguable points are emerging when comparing the Jewish nation to others.

Some scholars argue that the Jewish nation is primarily defined by its religious identity, positing that being Jewish is mostly a matter of religious belief and observance. From this viewpoint, Jews worldwide are united by their shared faith and religious practices, forming a nation defined by adherence to Judaism rather than geography or ancestry. Another perspective acknowledges diverse Jewish communities globally, viewing the global Jewish community as a transnational or global nation. This perspective emphasizes the interconnectedness and shared interests of Jews regardless of their geographic location, emphasizing the concept of a People of Israel rather than a strictly defined nation. Conversely, some argue that Jews of the diaspora constitute a distinct cultural and historical nation, highlighting shared traditions, customs, and a collective memory of persecution and survival. Advocates of this view underscore the importance of Jewish culture, heritage, and history as defining elements of a Jewish nation.

Without infringing on the domain of specialists in Judaism, and not claiming to be an expert on this subject, it seems fair to me to state here that the definition of the Jewish nation combines elements from all these perspectives.

Throughout history, Jewish communities residing in host countries have engaged in cultural exchanges with their respective societies, influencing and being influenced by local cultures. This dynamic interaction has given rise to a distinctive blend of traditions, customs, languages, culinary practices, music, art, and folklore within Jewish communities. Despite these influences, the Jews of the diaspora, in their everyday life and religion, share common values and traditions that stem from Jewish culture. The commonalities among Jewish communities residing within the borders of host countries for centuries underscore the fact that Jews are descendants of the Jewish people dispersed by the Romans in the first century C.E.

Anti-Semitism has played a significant role in uniting the Jews of the diaspora into a single nation and shaping their mentality. The origins of anti-Semitism are multifaceted, often rooted in feelings of inferiority or envy.[1] Winston Churchill acknowledged that some anti-Semitism stems from those who consider themselves less intelligent than Jews. Through centuries, envy, ironically linked to the high literacy rates of Jews, has also fueled anti-Semitism. As a 'people of the book,' Jews en masse continuously analyzed and debated the TORAH, contributing to their intellectual development. The ability to synthesize opposing concepts and understand practical issues of economics and management, coupled with adaptability, has led Jews to influential positions in social hierarchies. The freedom-loving tradition among Jews, especially noticeable in countries like Russia, where slavish submission is more common, has further contributed to anti-Semitism. Nevertheless, it is noteworthy that despite coexisting with Russians for two centuries, the Jewish community in this country did not assimilate the subservient mentality prevalent among local people. This divergence can be attributed not only to the annual commemoration of their historical enslavement in ancient Egypt during the Passover Seder but also to the consistent reinforcement of the idea that they were not a people destined for servitude. Slavery, much like idolatry, is deemed unnatural for the Jewish identity. Entrenched over centuries, this mindset has endured, remaining pertinent even in the present day—over three-quarters of a century since the Holocaust. Anti-Semitism, an affliction ingrained in our civilization, persists as a force preventing Jews from disconnecting from their roots. Paradoxically, this relentless reminder not only fortifies the cohesion of the Jewish nation but also propels them to be more competitive, productive, and innovative. Consequently, it contributes to their disproportionate success across various realms of human endeavor. A striking textbook

---

1 It is studied in great detail by Joseph Jacobs. See: Jacobs, Joseph. *Jewish contribution to civilization: an estimate*. The Jewish Publication Society of America. Philadelphia. 1919

illustration of this phenomenon lies in the statistics of Nobel Prize laureates: despite constituting a mere 0.2% of the global population, Jews have claimed 21% of the prestigious awards—100 times more than one would expect based on proportional representation.[2]

Jews find themselves in a unique situation as a nation that lost its independence and territory almost 2,000 years ago but has not disappeared like other nations in similar circumstances. Despite historical oppression and persecution, Jews have thrived and contributed to civilizations for centuries. With the onset of Jewish emancipation in the eighteenth century, Jews achieved success in various fields, including culture, where they developed *Jewish Architecture*.[3]

To define and assess this *Jewish Architecture*, it is essential to first deliberate on the subject of Architecture itself. In this chapter, we will explore various facets of architecture, considering their roles in defining *Jewish Architecture*.

---

2 See: Krasner, Jonathan B., Sarna, Jonathan D. *The History of the Jewish People: Ancient Israel to 1880s America*. Behrman House, Inc. 2006. p. 1.

3 In the mid-twentieth century a Jewish state, Israel, was reborn. Its achievements in the realm of architecture are a subject of the *Israel Architecture* study.

THE CREATION OF HABITAT. There are different approaches to defining architecture. Some architectural historians, laypeople, and even certain architects perceive and judge architectural works as sculptural objects, akin to pieces of art. They believe that the essence of architecture lies in its form, asserting that architects' primary task is to enhance the aesthetic appeal of buildings. This reduction of architecture to an art form places it alongside painting, sculpture, literature, theater, and other artistic disciplines.

As a result, these people treat the history of architecture in the same manner as the history of art, considering it a narrative of evolving artistic styles.

Nevertheless, the architectural object extends beyond mere aesthetics of attractiveness or ugliness. When individuals in the USA, for example, purchase a Cape Cod house (or for that matter, Georgian, Queen Anne, French Revival, or Contemporary), they likely appreciate the architectural aesthetics of the house, especially when viewing its images in coffee table books. However, their interest extends beyond visual appeal to practical considerations of livability. Take, for instance, the one-and-a-half-story Cape Cod house with a central stairway, originating in New England. Its famous minimalistic and elegant exterior, featuring mostly shingle siding and wooden shutters, was not conceived as a piece of art but rather as a response to the local extreme winter climate. Similarly, in Central Asian residential architecture, the charming arrangement of rooms of varying heights around a courtyard was not designed for picturesque effects but to facilitate necessary natural airflow and ventilation in local houses.

In both cases—the Cape Cod house and Central Asian assemblies—purely vernacular architectural achievements came into being because the primary purpose of architecture lies not in the embellishment of buildings but in the creation of suitable human environments. 'Appropriate' in this context can range from simple functionality to high sophistication, depending on the specific circumstances.

A notable example is the Gothic cathedral, a magnificent creation intended to establish a soaring sacred space filled with light (Illus. 1.1.1). However, over time, this invention became canonized as an art style, with its elements being employed purely for ornamental purposes. As an architect and theoretician Moisei Ginzburg observed, a similar transformation occurred with the arches originally used by the Etruscans in sewers, bridges, and monumental gates across various locations, which later became decorative motifs in the Renaissance epoch.[4]

So, why do some people still perceive architecture as a form of art? They are misled, likely, because numerous arguments support such an approach. Architects, like artists, incorporate aesthetic considerations into their work. They engage in a creative process, utilizing subconscious and associative thinking. Moreover, there is a temptation to assess the results of architects' activities based on their sculptural qualities. Many treatises have been penned on architecture as an art form, and architectural theoreticians have adhered to this concept for centuries. Multiple generations of architects and architecture critics have been raised with this perspective, and it has left its mark on the field.

However, this hasn't always been the case. In Western society, the pure aesthetic approach to architecture can be traced back to the Renaissance, a period in European architecture that witnessed a revival and development of certain

4 Ginzburg, Moisei. *Style and Epoch*. The MIT Press, 1983.

1.1.1. Chartres Cathedral. Interior. Photo credit: Dominic Arizona Bonuccelli

elements of ancient Greek and Roman thought and material culture between the thirteenth and early seventeenth centuries. During this time, a limited set of structure types formed the architectural canon: fortifications, churches or temples, palaces and mansions of feudal and church nobility, and entertainment buildings. Renaissance thinkers aimed to bring visual order to these diverse structures, emulating the Greco-Roman style that European intellectuals had recently rediscovered.

Over the last approximately 200 years, a different understanding of architecture—one predating the Renaissance—began to reemerge. In the mid-nineteenth century, critiques were raised against Classicist (or Academic) architecture. Instead of viewing architecture purely as an aesthetic pursuit, proponents of these new views sought to recover the original, pre-Renaissance perspective of architecture as the application of available technology to serve human needs by creating and organizing space. While the Renaissance vision distinguished between building and architecture, the emerging modern view aimed to create a unified definition, shifting architecture from the application of ornaments to a building to a creative approach to building.

Since ancient times, architecture has been perceived as a means of creating habitat. The first-century B.C.E. Roman architect and engineer Vitruvius described architecture as having three essential characteristics: utility, strength, and beauty.[5] This understanding implies that art is one of the natural components of architecture. Architecture diverges from the work of artists (painters, sculptors, writers, poets, and others) in that it involves creating the material environment—the habitat. Also, unlike art, architecture cannot be realized without a close interrelationship with the client: the project's financier and end-user. While artists may work sometimes with patrons or state institutions, architects invariably always do so. An exception is paper architecture, a form of art prac-ticed by some architects.

According to proponents of the contemporary view on architecture, an ~~architect not only~~ organizes and allo-

cates space and constructs its enclosure but also envisions and organizes human activity within it.[6] The functional and formal components of the design are inseparable. Reflecting on a famous twentieth-century architectural maxim, Frank Lloyd Wright noted that "'form follows function' is mere dogma until you realize the higher truth that form and function are one."[7] This paradigm has shaped Western architecture over the past century.

The perception of architecture as primarily an aesthetic pursuit often distorts the role of the architect, reducing it to the decoration of buildings. Therefore, when attempting to define *Jewish Architecture*, it is crucial to acknowledge that the discussion pertains not to stylistic elements of architecture but rather to the man-made physical environment.[8]

---

5   Vitruvius called architecture the 'mother of all arts,' and reminded the reader that the original Ancient Grecian meaning of the word architect was 'the main builder.' See: Vitruvius. *On Architecture*. Harvard University Press. 1914. Bk 1. Ch. 3.2. p.17.

6   See: Loos, Adolf. *On Architecture*. Ariadne Press. 2007; Ginzburg, Moisei. *Style and Epoch*. The MIT Press, 1983; Harries, Karsten. *The Ethical Function of Architecture*. The MIT Press, 1997; http://www.mom.arq.ufmg.br/mom/arq_interface/2a_aula/loos_architecture.pdf.

7   Wright, Frank Lloyd. *The Natural House*. Horizon Press, New York. 1954. P. 20

8   Of course, stylistic elements, the visual features that give a building its unique character (the shape, size, and proportion of the building, as well as the materials used, and the decorative details) are an important part

DUALITIES IN ARCHITECTURE. The subject of architecture could be represented also as a set of dualistic compromises. First of all, there is a compromise between the client and the architect. The presence of two initiators in any architectural project—the client and the architect—is a fundamental component of the subject of architecture. The clients, often with the architect's participation, develop the project's program and finance its implementation. The architects propose options based on their understanding of the challenges presented by the program. Ideally, both the client and the architect share a common vision for the project, but often, this ideal scenario is not realized. The reality is that neither the client nor the architect can have everything they desire in the project, leading to unavoidable trade-offs. Although these trade-offs can be challenging, they are inevitable, resulting in a building developed as a compromise solution.

During the project's development, the architect and the client must also navigate the contradiction between the building's function and its formal appearance. This compromise between function and form arises from the dualism inherent in architectural design. While the functional and formal components of the design are inseparable, typically, the function dictates the form. However, the form of the building can itself serve a functional purpose also, particularly in places of worship or a corporation headquarters. The quality of the compromise between the requirements of function and form hinges on the architect's skill and understanding of the significance of these architectural components in each case.

Among all the arts, sculpture is the closest to architecture. In every architectural project, there is an element of sculpture. Its presence varies based on the building type and the creative impulse of the architect, reflecting their conceptual approach to shaping. Moreover, for the same architect, sculpture can assume a more significant role, for instance, in a religious building compared to a warehouse. Similarly, office buildings designed by different architects, such as Frank Lloyd Wright and Mies van der Rohe, can exhibit substantial differences.

---

of the man–made physical environment—architecture. Their role in architecture is multifaceted, encompassing aesthetics, cultural context, symbolism, and the expression of architectural ideas and ideals.

Art is just one facet of architecture. Architecture stands apart from art not only due to the client's participation in its results and the resolution of function versus form contradictions but also through the solution of problems related to selecting and allocating space from the environment and its organization. An architect is not merely a decorator of life but its organizer. Unlike the sculptor, the architect not only organizes and allocates space but also orchestrates the processes of human activity within it while constructing its shell. Simultaneously, the natural foundation of the architectural configuration serves as both a utilitarian component of the structure and an aesthetic element of the form. This is how art seamlessly integrates into architecture.

Throughout the history of architecture, there have been numerous instances where the compromise between function and form tilts towards the side of form, leading an architectural project to almost entirely adopt a sculptural essence. St. Basil's Cathedral in Moscow, Russia (Illus.1.2.1 and 1.2.2), serves as an example, where there is almost no space for worship. On the contrary, in cases of balanced compromise, such as the Chapel of Notre Dame du Haut in Ronchamp, France (Illus.1.2.3 and 1.2.4), designed by the architect Le Corbusier, the structure, despite its sculptural nature, effectively fulfills its functional purpose.

Hence, when contemplating the design of diverse structures—be it a factory shop, a residential building, or a museum—we subconsciously apply an equally stringent but entirely different criterion for assessing their degree of sculptural quality.

Since the sculptural aspect of architecture is inherently artistic and, as such, influenced by contemporary art styles that significantly shape architectural forms, it is pertinent to briefly divert and delve into the concept of style in architecture. This exploration is necessary because, at times, the architectures of various nations are labeled merely as different styles of architecture, such as Japanese style, Arab style, and so forth. This intriguing subject will be the focus of the upcoming chapter.

1.2.1. St. Basil's Cathedral. Moscow. Russia. 1555. Street view.
Photo credit: photoputeshestviya.ru

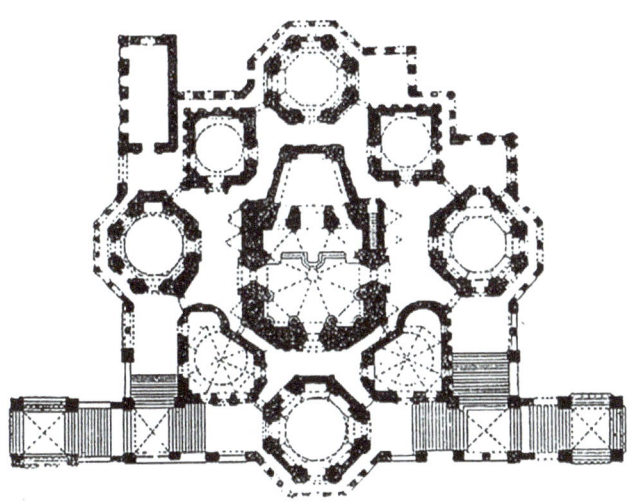

1.2.2. St. Basil's Cathedral. Moscow, Russia. 1555. Floor Plan. Photo credit: public domain

1.2.3. Le Corbusier. Chapel of Notre Dame du Haut. Ronchamp. France. 1950-1955.
Photo credit: ALAMY

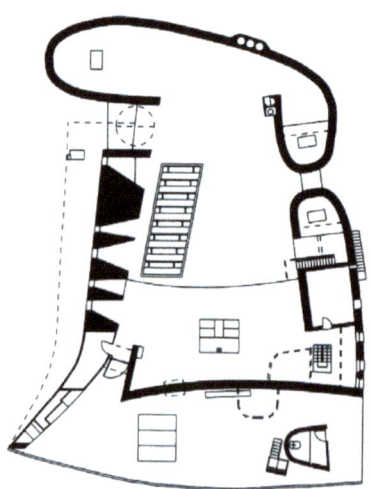

1.2.4. Le Corbusier. Chapel of Notre Dame du Haut. Ronchamp. France. 1950-1955.
Floor plan. Photo credit: Nekha Thomas

Chapter 2. Function, Style, and Epoch in Architecture

In the first chapter, to delve into the concept of *Jewish Architecture*, we defined the broader subject of architecture and explored its dualistic nature. Within discussions about *Jewish Architecture*, some scholars and the informed public utilize the terms 'Jewish Identity' and 'Jewish style.' These expressions specifically pertain to the sculptural aspect of architecture, which is intricately linked to themes of fashion, style, and architectural epochs. This chapter aims to examine these terms and their significance in shaping national architecture.

FASHION AND STYLE. It goes without saying that a building must fulfill its designated purpose, whether serving as a home, school, hospital, factory, museum, place of worship, or any other building type. Additionally, it is common knowledge that architecture extends beyond mere functionality. One of its fundamental facets is the physical form of a building. This formal component of architecture—the language of architecture for each nation—has evolved over centuries, influenced not only by the intended use, materials, and technologies of each historical era but also by the building's interaction with its environment, the climate of the nation's land, its people's traditions, and way of life.[1]

Simultaneously, the form of a building, its sculptural component, is considered an art form. As such, it adheres to ever-changing fashions and styles—two concepts often used interchangeably in the field of architecture. However, it is crucial to remember that art is just one facet of architecture, alongside function, design elements, structure, economics, and more. When referencing style in architecture, we are addressing its artistic aspect—the artistic style of building. This nuance also applies to the concept of fashion in architecture, where using the terms 'artistic fashion' and 'artistic style' might be more precise than 'fashion' and 'style.'

---

1   This subject will be discussed in greater detail in the next chapter.

There is a subtle difference between the two. Artistic fashion in architecture pertains to contemporary trends in design and construction. It is often driven by new technologies, materials, and the desire to create something novel and captivating. Fashionable details may include the use of specific materials, colors, or ornamentation. While eye-catching and innovative, artistic fashion can be fleeting and may quickly become outdated.

On the other hand, artistic style in architecture is a more enduring concept than fashion. It encompasses the totality of space, form, and decoration—sometimes described as architectural language. A building's artistic style is typically defined by numerous features of the era in which it was constructed, including architectural and art movements that influenced its design.

Distinguishing between fashion and style is not always straightforward for contemporaries. To illustrate, consider the façades of buildings associated with the so-called post-modern movement in architecture during the late twentieth century. Designed by renowned individuals such as Michael Graves, Frank Gehry, Ricardo Bofill, Charles Moore, James Stirling, and Stanley Tigerman, among others, these buildings exemplify both talent and the influence of the architectural fashion of the time.

If we explore such buildings as the Portland Building in Oregon (Illus. 2.1.1), Guggenheim Museum in Bilbao, Spain (Illus. 2.2.1) by Frank Gehry, the Ville Nouvelle of Marne-la Vallée (Illus. 2.2.2, 2.2.3, 2.2.4 and 2.2.5) by Ricardo Bofill, the Piazza d'Italia in New Orleans (Illus. 2.2.6) by Charles Moore, Num-ber One Poultry in London (Illus. 2.2.7, 2.2.8 and 2.2.9) by James Stirling, and Daisy House (Illus. 2.2.10 and 2.2.11) by Stanley Tigerman, we will see that these structures are not indicative of a specific artistic style in architecture but rather embody architectural fashions, driven by the individualistic impulses of their creators.

In architecture, the style reflects the culmination of numerous trials and errors during the development of architectural types within a particular epoch of the architectural history of a nation or region. The 'trial and error' concept is a fundamental aspect characterizing each epoch. However, it is crucial to distinguish between style as an artistic notion and the broader aspects of architecture. Defining architecture solely by its artistic style is limiting as it focuses

2.1.1. Michael Graves. The Portland Building in Oregon.
USA. 1982. Photo credit: Susan Grant Lewin

2.2.1. Frank Gehry. Guggenheim Museum. Bilbao, Spain. 1997. Interior. Photo by author

2.2.2. Ricardo Bofill. Les Espaces Abraxas Marne la Valle. Paris, France.1983.
Photo credit: RBTA

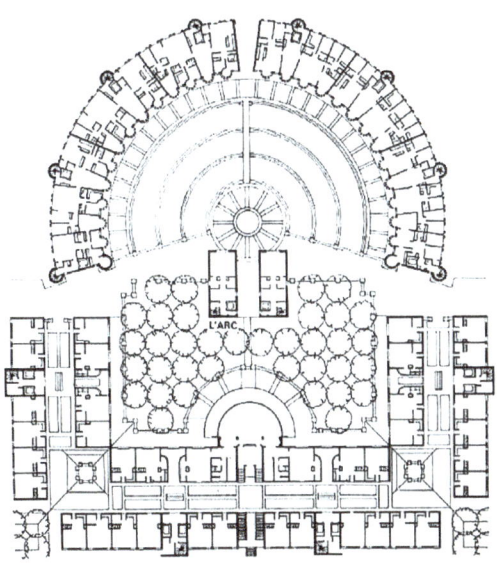

2.2.3. Ricardo Bofill. Les Espaces Abraxas Marne la Valle. Paris, France. 1983.
Floor plan. Photo credit: RBTA

2.2.4. Ricardo Bofill. Les Espaces Abraxas Marne la Valle. Paris, France. 1983.
Photo credit: RBTA

2.2.5. Ricardo Bofill. Les Espaces Abraxas Marne la Valle. Paris, France. 1983.
Photo credit: RBTA

2.2.6. Charles Moore. Piazza d'Italia. New Orleans, Louisiana. 1978. Photo credit: Pinterest

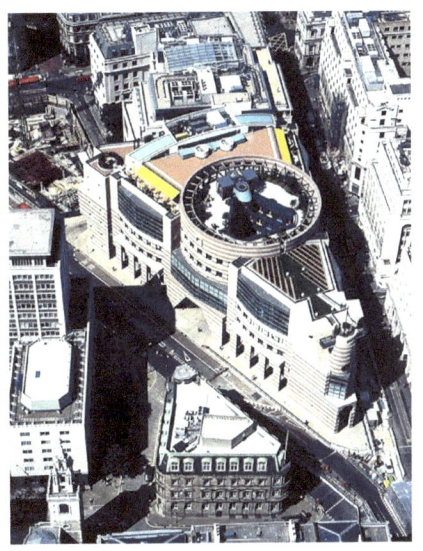

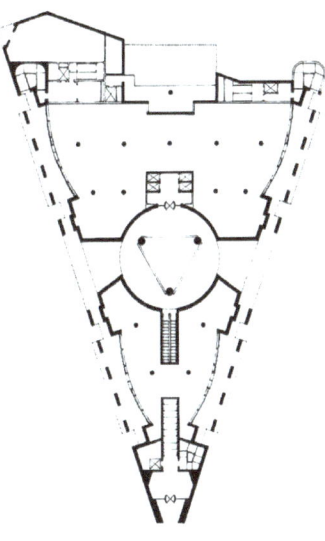

2.2.7. James Stirling. Number one Poultry. London. UK. 1997. Birds View. Photo credit: James Stirling/ Michael Wilford fonds

2.2.8. James Stirling. Number one Poultry. London, UK. 1997. Floor plan. Photo credit: James Stirling/Michael Wilford fonds

2.2.9. James Stirling. Number one Gallery. London. UK. 1997. Photo credit: James Stirling/ Michael Wilford fonds

2.2.10. Stanley Tigerman. Daisy House. Porter Beach, Indiana. USA. 1979. Street view. Photo credit: Tigerman McCurry

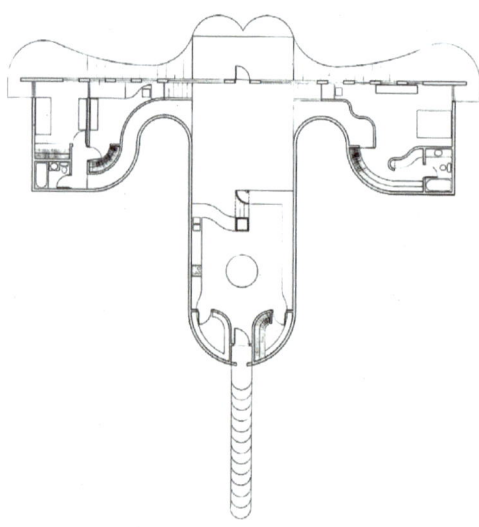

2.2.11. Stanley Tigerman. Daisy House. Porter Beach, Indiana. USA. 1979. Floor plan. Photo credit: Tigerman McCurry

only on the sculptural component of architecture. While inseparable from function, construction, and materials, the concept of style should be used with care, either explicitly emphasizing its artistic connotation or refraining from its use altogether.

Stylistic elements play a pivotal role in architecture, contributing to aesthetics, cultural context, symbolism, and the expression of architectural ideas. These elements serve various purposes, such as conveying meaning and reflecting the building's purpose, its owner, or cultural background. Stylistic elements also contribute to creating a sense of place within a community and enhance the overall beauty of a space. Constituting the sculptural facet of architecture, they encompass the building's shape, size, proportion, materials, and decorative details. These visual features collectively contribute to a building's unique character.

The shape of a building can evoke drama or tranquility; for instance, a triangular roof imparts a sense of movement, while a circular structure conveys peace and tranquility. Size can make a statement, with a large building suggesting power and authority, while a small one creates a sense of intimacy and warmth. Proportion influences perceptions of stability or airiness, with a large base and a small top suggesting stability and a small base and a large top conveying lightness and airiness. The choice of materials, such as stone for permanence and strength or glass for lightness and transparency, can create a sense of warmth, coolness, luxury, or simplicity. Decorative details, like carved gargoyles or stained-glass windows, add interest and personality, while clean lines and unadorned surfaces evoke a sense of modern design.

All facets of fashion and style play their role in defining national architecture. Their significance can be traced through two major epochs in European architecture, commonly referred to as 'styles': Gothic and Renaissance. These epochs have left a lasting impact on the subsequent development of world architecture.

GOTHIC. Gothic architecture emerged in response to the burgeoning populations and increasing wealth of North European cities. The need to accommodate larger numbers of pilgrims in churches led to the development of new types of monumental religious structures, exemplified by cathedrals like

2.3.1. Canterbury Cathedral. Canterbury. Kent, England. 1070-1834. Street view. Photo credit: public domain

Canterbury (Illus. 2.3.1.) and Chartres (Illus. 2.3.2, 2.2.3 and 2.3.4). Concurrent theological doctrines emphasized the expression of local grandeur, fostering a desire for greater height and increased lighting. To achieve this, larger windows became essential, resulting in a reduction of wall space and advancements in vaults and flying buttresses. In Medieval Europe, architectural endeavors predominantly centered around robust stone structures. However, as the demand for expansive religious edifices grew, a novel construction approach emerged—the frame. This method, eventually labeled as 'Gothic,' revolutionized the construction of towering buildings by enabling the use of thinner walls. Therefore, Gothic architecture evolved directly in response to changing societal conditions. However, elements of its architectural language became later fashionable and transformed into the so-called 'Gothic style.' Gothic architecture encompasses more than just façades with pointed arches, flying buttresses, and enormous stained-glass windows; it represents a holistic approach to function, space, and construction methods. In other words, the term 'Gothic style'

2.3.2. Chartres Cathedral. Chartres, France, 1194. Flying-buttresses.
Photo credit: chartressidedetail

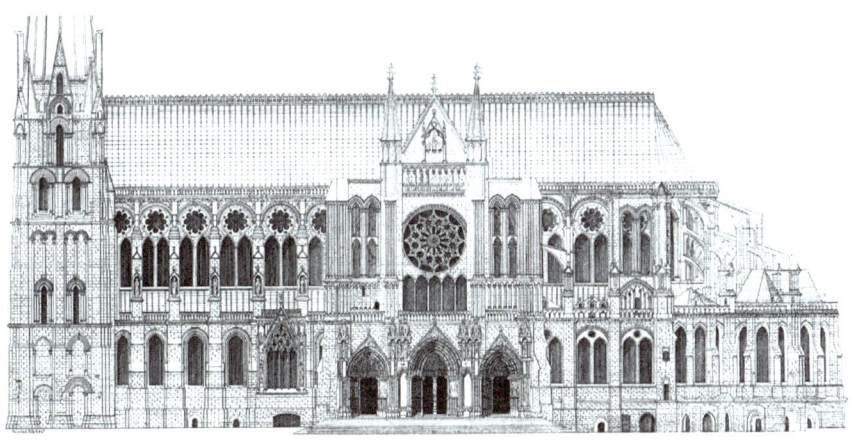

2.3.3. Chartres Cathedral. Chartres, France. 1194. Facade drawing.
Photo credit: chartressidedetail

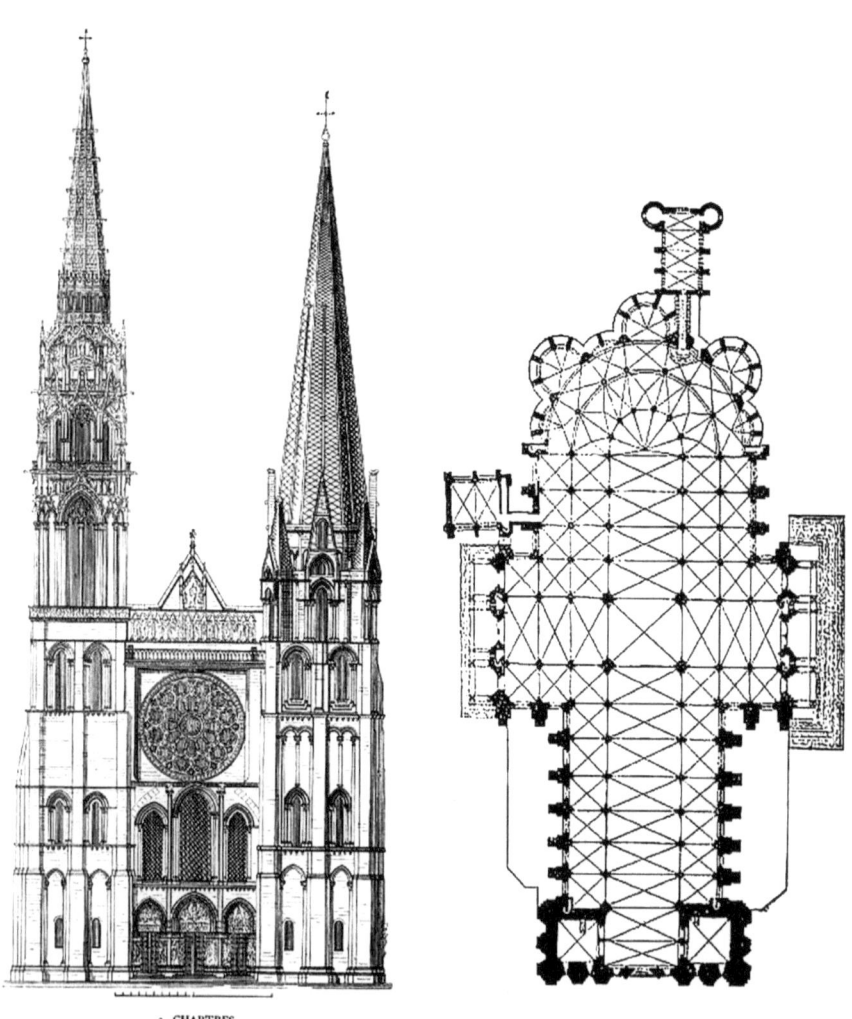

2.3.4. Chartres Cathedral. Chartres, France. 1194. Facade and plan drawings. Photo credit: chartressidedetail, chartreselevation

encompasses an entire architectural epoch, better referred to as the 'Gothic Epoch.'

It is worth noting that Gothic architecture incorporated artistic forms from earlier architectural traditions. For instance, it drew inspiration from Islamic architecture, as evident in features like the pointed arch. Additionally, it exhibited strong influences from Late Roman and Byzantine artistic styles, particularly seen in using capitals adorned with serpentine lines and naturalistic forms. Furthermore, traces of Romanesque architecture can be observed in the abundant use of stone within Gothic structures.

New building materials, building technology, and a new philosophical assessment of reality, which lead to a change in societal aesthetic preferences, give rise to new architectural forms. However, sometimes the next direction in architectural shaping arises at the whim of individuals and can impact an entire architectural epoch. A textbook example is the Eiffel Tower, which Parisians initially met with hostility but now they are gratified by it.

As discussed earlier, among contemporary architectural theorists, there is a tendency to sometimes conflate architecture with art and subsequently apply the concept of artistic style to architecture. It is worth noting that this conflation was prevalent from the Renaissance times when architecture was universally regarded as an art form until the twentieth century.[2] During this period, architecture incorporated various art styles, and art historians and the general public relied on this classification to evaluate architectural works. This approach has had a lasting impact on today's researchers as well. Since the Renaissance era had a profound impact on architectural thought and practice for several centuries and still influences architectural discourse, let us delve into it in greater detail.

RENAISSANCE. Architecture is the art of creating habitat, involving the design and construction of structures. However, during the Renaissance period in European history (thirteenth–seventeenth century), architecture was

---

2 The term 'Renaissance' was introduced in the nineteenth century by French historian Jules Michelet, to describe a period in European history that spanned roughly from the thirteenth to the seventeenth century. The word "Renaissance" is derived from the French word meaning "rebirth" and reflects the renewed interest in classical learning, arts, and culture that characterized this era.

perceived as the art applied to buildings, with a focus on achieving beauty in erected structures. This equating of architecture with art meant that the criterion for architects' work was predominantly centered on artistic considerations. The goal of architecture became defined as creating unifying compositions and orderly façades. Even as some building types evolved over the next four hundred years, developments similar to Islamic decorative architecture happened. The walls of buildings were seen as canvases for the application of Classical orders, which themselves became more complex and ornate.

Renaissance architecture owed much of its presence to the popularity of talented artists who ventured into architecture also. Unlike the Gothic Epoch, the Renaissance did not emerge from the advent of new building materials or construction methods or the necessity to construct new types of buildings. Instead, it arose from a demand for a new aesthetic fashion that aligned with the tastes of the elite, particularly the church and wealthy feudal lords. This era witnessed significant innovations in the sculptural component of architecture, influencing both building exteriors and interiors.

The Renaissance, with its various modifications, left a lasting cultural impact on European society from the thirteenth to the twentieth century. It was a time of considerable change and upheaval in Europe, marked by cultural and intellectual transformations, a shift from the medieval worldview to a more humanistic and individualistic approach.

The Renaissance marked a revival of interest in ancient Greek and Roman literature, philosophy, and art, making significant contributions to both the arts and sciences. Renowned figures in literature, politics, and science, such as Dante Alighieri, Francesco Petrarca, Leonardo da Vinci, Niccolò Machiavelli, Nicolaus Copernicus, Miguel de Cervantes, and Galileo Galilei, played pivotal roles during this period. Philosophers like Thomas More and influential writers like William Shakespeare also left their mark.

In the realm of visual arts, sculpture, and architecture, notable names such as Michelangelo Buonarroti, Raphael, Giovanni Bernini, Filippo Brunelleschi, and Donato Bramante emerged. While artists and thinkers aspired to surpass cultural achievements of the ancient world, Renaissance architects, many of whom were originally painters and sculptors, drew inspiration from the façades of ancient classical architects' buildings.

Despite exceptions like Brunelleschi and Bramante, who contributed iconic structures like the dome of Florence Cathedral (Illus. 2.4.1) and Tempietto in Rome (Illus. 2.4.2), respectively, architects did not typically hold a leading role in the Renaissance architectural scene. Instead, the forefront was often occupied by artists. The patrons (read—partners) of architects, the new elite, viewed architecture as an art form and frequently turned to painters and sculptors for commissions.

The significance of major clients, such as Lorenzo de Medici, Popes Leo X and Paul III for Michelangelo, and Cardinal Borghese and Popes Innocent X and Alexander VII for Bernini, played a crucial role in shaping Renaissance architecture. Without such influential patrons with specific insights into architecture, Michelangelo might not have ventured into architecture at all,[3]

and the Baroque art style might not have emerged. Nevertheless, collectively, all these figures and their accomplishments helped shape the Renaissance as a remarkable era of intellectual and artistic flourishing, leaving a lasting legacy.

However, the Renaissance epoch cannot be deemed as an era of progress in architecture. Despite the captivating names associated with Renaissance architecture, featuring luminaries such as Brunelleschi, Bramante, Alberti, Palladio, Vignola, Michelangelo, Raphael, and Bernini, the Renaissance architecture, particularly from the Cinquecento era onward, can be perceived as a step backward. While as a cultural phenomenon, the Renaissance did embody a fresh philosophical perspective, in architecture, it failed to introduce innovative building types that could mirror evolving societal conditions, incorporate novel construction materials and methods, or manifest new architectural forms. Instead, Renaissance architecture emerged as a purely artistic style, shaped by the prevailing artistic trends and the whims of patrons.

---

[3] Michelangelo never considered himself an architect, which he was not. At different points in his life, he wrote, "I am not an architect" (Wilde, Johannes. *Michelangelo and His Studio*. United Kingdom: British Museum Publications for the Trustees of the British Museum, 1953. p. 109f), and "it is not my profession" (*Le lettere di Michelangelo Buonarroti by Michelangelo Buonarroti*. EBook-No.46599. p.431). Michelangelo understood that he was an artist.

2.4.1. Filippo Brunelleschi. Cathedral of Santa-Maria del Fiore. Florence, Italy. 1436. Duomo. Photo credit: Charles W. Warren

2.4.2. Donato Bramante. Tempietto. San Pietro in Motorio courtyard. Rome, Italy. 1502. Photo credit: © marpet/Fotolia

Unfortunately, the legacy of applying the concept of style to architecture, which gained prominence during the Renaissance, still persists in architectural history references. Paying tribute to the Renaissance, these sources often define architectural epochs as so-called 'architectural styles' based on decorative details found on building façades, perpetuating a classification that oversimplifies the complexities of architectural evolution.

The Renaissance architecture and its derivatives, appear to be the dead-end side branches of the development of Western architecture. During the Baroque era, architecture was turned into sculpture, but at other times of the Renaissance, architecture was simply engaged in decorating buildings. These tangential branches of the development of history eventually faded away; in the case of the Renaissance, it took centuries for these so-called styles to become museum artifacts. Considering them as enduring architectural achievements seems to be a common misconception, akin to beliefs that attribute climate change primarily to an increase in methane emissions from cows.

In contrast, the contemporary architectural paradigm has undergone a significant transformation. Echoing pre-Renaissance times, architecture is now widely acknowledged as a distinct discipline separate from art. While we can use artistic criteria to assess works from the Renaissance and its derivatives, it's essential to recognize the somewhat tenuous connection. When evaluating buildings from that era within their context, we primarily acknowledge their cultural and artistic significance within our heritage rather than evaluating them purely as architecture.

An architect strives to achieve organic integration of function, space, and shell of the structure. Each of these components has a different weight in various structures, according to their use. At the same time, we could conditionally divide habitat structures into several categories, including residential, religious, industrial, educational, recreational, and entertainment, to name a few. An architect could emphasize the form, for instance, in a museum building more than in a residential building, where the most important task is the functional organization of space.

Overemphasizing the role of art in the design of a building can sometimes lead to the transformation of architecture into mere sculpture. Renowned architects like Daniel Libeskind, along with his former mentor Peter Eisenman, engaged in projects that experiment with the spatial aspects of spaces, aiming to evoke emotions in users. This approach is purely aesthetic and sculptural in nature, which finds justification only in the context of such buildings as museums, churches, synagogues, and similar types where the form of the structure is an integral part of its function and conveys meaningful symbolism.

However, this artistic emphasis becomes less justified when architects prioritize it excessively in residential buildings. In such cases, it can devolve into an attempt to interpret architecture solely as sculpture. Frequently, architects undertake this transformation with the approval of the client. This trend is observable in the works of architects like Frank Gehry (Illus. 2.4.3 and 2.4.4), Zaha Hadid (Illus. 2.4.5 and 2.4.6), and others, where the functional aspects are at times overlooked. Perhaps these endeavors should be seen as experimental works, akin to other extremes in design where the focus is exclusively on function, as seen in the early Bauhaus residential buildings. Striking a balance

2.4.3. Frank Gehry. The Dancing House. Prague, Czech Republic, 1994.
Photo credit: Brian Hammonds/Getty Images

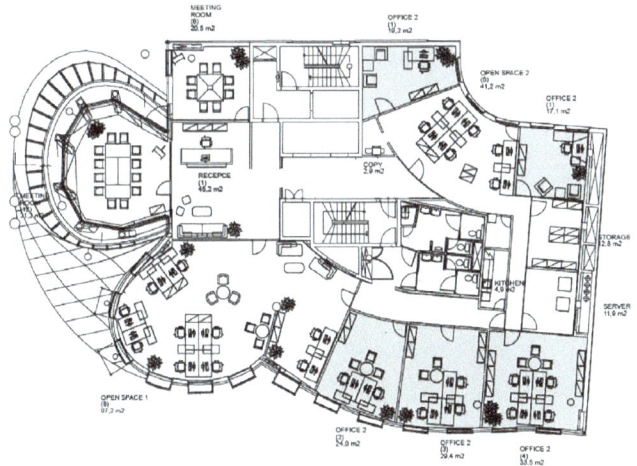

2.4.4. Frank Gehry. The Dancing House. Prague, Czech Republic, 1994. Floor plan.
Photo credit: nowshinmatin

2.4.5. Zaha Hadid. CityLife Milano residential Complex, 2014. Street View.
Photo credit: Simon Garcia

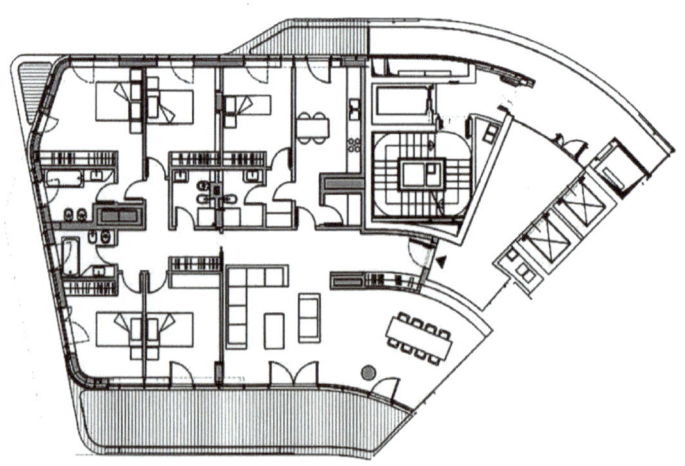

2.4.6. Zaha Hadid. CityLife Milano residential Complex, 2014. Floor plan.
Photo credit: Pinterest

between artistic expression and functional requirements remains a critical consideration in architectural design.

We are familiar with and study the history of architecture through preserved or excavated buildings. These include religious buildings, such as Buddhist temples, Egyptian tombs, Greek or Roman temples, as well as local noble palaces. Sculptural facets of architecture often serve a functional purpose within these structures. Therefore, we need to consider the overabundance of intricate details in these buildings and acknowledge the biases in their design toward embellishment.

Undoubtedly, the shape of a building and the intricacies of its façades and interiors play a significant role in architecture. However, when viewed from the perspective of the client and the end-user, whether it be a residential, industrial, religious, or museum structure, the primary concern is whether the building effectively fulfills its intended purpose. A case in point is the groundbreaking extension to the Art Museum in Bilbao. Despite its visual allure, this extension cannot be deemed a wholly successful architectural work as, judging by this book author's experience, visitors to the museum may feel dizziness in its uneven and unconventional spaces. Intentionally or not, the architect devised the building as a striking piece of sculpture, and its aesthetic appeal as a sculpture played a crucial role in revitalizing the city's economy.

Certainly, the aesthetic appeal of architecture is widely acknowledged, but the question lies in the criteria used to evaluate this visual appeal. In contrast, it may seem like a purely subjective matter, but societies throughout history have consistently formulated specific notions of beauty at each stage of their development. Modern perspectives on beauty often diverge from those held centuries ago. Consequently, incorporating archaic forms by contemporary architects can sometimes appear awkward. When modern buildings adopt Renaissance or Gothic details on their façades, leading to what is termed 'Gothic Revival,' it should be recognized as a misrepresentation rather than an authentic representation of Gothic architecture. This principle extends to other architectural revivals as well. The challenge lies in striking a balance between appreciating historical elements and avoiding the misrepresentation of artistic styles in the contemporary architectural context.

In literature, when referring to buildings constructed in a so-called 'Jewish style,' it often implies structures adorned with elements of the 'Moorish Revival.' For the 'Moorish Revival,' the distinctiveness lies in its decorative elements. Removing these art elements from the façade would result in a structure that is indistinguishable from others of a similar nature. It is crucial to clarify that Jewish identity and Jewishness do not inherently correspond with the 'Moorish Revival.' This artistic style in architecture primarily involves decorative elements and does not define the essence of Jewish culture or identity. A more in-depth exploration of this topic will be provided later in Chapter 6.

Outlining *Jewish Architecture*, we shall remember that the peak of notable architectural advancements during a particular cultural period within society gives birth to a new architecture. This goes beyond encompassing merely stylistic elements related to the sculptural aspect of architecture. It also involves the introduction of new building types, innovative materials, construction techniques, fresh approaches to organizing living spaces, and the evolution of aesthetic beliefs. Rather than labeling the outcomes of these advancements as mere styles, it appears more fitting to characterize them as epochs in architecture.

The evolution of a diverse array of fashions, forms, and artistic styles in architecture is deeply connected to national traditions, the introduction of new building types, and advancements in building materials and construction methods. This intricate process contributes significantly to the shaping of national architecture. Such developments can be observed throughout history on a global scale, spanning from Japan and India to Europe and America. A more thorough examination of this topic will be conducted in the next chapter.

Chapter 3. National Architecture

In previous chapters, we delved into the topic of architecture, exploring its elements and the way they influence artistic style within national architecture. On the flip side, the national architecture of any nation is a totality of structures on this nation's territory. To understand how the delineation of *Jewish Architecture* aligns with this definition, discussions in this chapter will delve into the centuries-long development of building art of other nations on their respective territories, commencing with an examination of their vernacular architecture.

THE ROLE OF VERNACULAR ARCHITECTURE. The architecture of any country boasts a rich and extensive history, reaching back to the earliest developments on its territory. Across the centuries, vernacular architecture has experienced numerous epochs in each country and region, each uniquely mirroring the prevailing culture and values of its time. Throughout these periods, distinctive sculptural forms and architectural details emerged, aligning with prevalent fashions and styles.

The evolution of a nation's architecture is most visibly embodied in its residential structures, spanning from primitive caves and huts to contemporary residential skyscrapers. Residential, or—vernacular —architecture stands at the core of a nation's architectural development. Housing architecture encapsulates crucial elements of national architecture, including traditions, building materials, technology, and aesthetic preferences, collectively defining the architectural identity of a nation.

The term 'vernacular architecture' pertains to the local, non-monumental building traditions of specific communities within a country. This aspect of architecture developed concurrently with more prominent structures, such as religious buildings, where sculptural elements played a significant role in function. Sometimes it leads to misconceptions about the genuine influence of local conditions on a country's architecture. While the function and form of vernacular buildings varied considerably based on geographical regions and cultural influences, they generally shared certain common features.

To comprehend an architectural epoch in any country, one must study its vernacular architecture. This architecture is the only true instrument to measure the developments and achievements of the country's architecture. It contains the 'genetic code' of any nation's architecture. Most of it exemplifying elements we could find in other types of structures developed later, from temples and churches to civic buildings, libraries, enclosed marketplaces, and sports halls, to name a few. In other words—in all representatives of the nation's national architecture.

The national architecture of each country serves as a testament to the ingenuity and creativity of the people who have inhabited these regions for centuries. Jewish diaspora resided in most of the countries of the civilized world. These countries' architecture affected Jewish culture and, in return, Jewish culture influenced their architecture. Exploring this is necessary to define *Jewish Architecture*. To do it, first, the unique architectural features in the development of national architecture should be studied and illuminated.

Specific features of national architecture are developed through the history of the architecture of each nation during a series of changing epochs. The appearance of each of these epochs is due to the changing social environment, the development of new materials and methods, and new aesthetical views.

JAPANESE ARCHITECTURE as any other nation's art of building reflects the country's unique cultural, social, and environmental factors. The geographical features of Japan, including its mountains, erupting volcanoes, and frequent earthquakes, along with changing economic conditions and cultural developments, have profoundly influenced the evolution of various architectural epochs in that country. Each of them has contributed to the rich tapestry of Japanese architecture, reflecting the country's history, and culture, and changing societal needs over time. Over time, in traditional vernacular Japanese architecture, the most typical elements of it were crystalized: flexible spaces, open corridors that surround traditional Japanese houses—engawas, steeply pitched roofs with large upturned eaves, and courtyards–gardens,

3.1.1. Samurai Residence. Japan.
Photo credit: Tristan Scholze

3.1.2. Gassho-zukuri houses. Japan
Photo credit: public domain

3.1.3. Gassho-zukuri house. Ogimachi.
Shirakawa-go, Japan.
Photo credit: Luke Robinson

as an essential component of Japanese architecture. Other distinctive features of Japanese architecture were formed also, such as materiality. It is represented in the incorporation of natural materials such as wood, bamboo, paper, and clay, and the modular design system, which is based on tatami mats. The development of all these elements of Japanese architecture during the centuries was a direct result of the influence of local traditions, climate, available construction materials, and methods. It is exemplified in traditional Minka residences (Illus.3.1.1). They have low, thatched roofs, wooden frames, and earthen walls. However, Gassho-zukuri farmhouses (Illus.3.1.2 and 3.1.3) located in the Shirakawa-go and Gokayama regions were designed to withstand heavy snowfall. They feature steep thatched roofs and large open spaces for silkworm cultivation.

During the Yayoi epoch (300 B.C.E.– 300 C.E.), marked by the introduction of rice cultivation and metalworking, houses featured raised floors and thatched roofs, as reflected in the Shinto Shrine (Illus. 3.1.4). Simple clay huts became more prevalent during this period. The Asuka era (538 C.E.–710 C.E.) witnessed the introduction of Buddhism from the Asian continent.

This influx influenced Japanese architecture significantly, evident in structures like the Horyuji Temple (Illus. 3.1.5), characterized by traditional wooden construction. The Nara epoch (710 C.E.–794 C.E.) was notable for the construction of grand Buddhist temples, pagodas, and palaces, exemplified by Todaiji Temple (Illus.3.1.6). Moving into the Heian period (794 C.E.–1185 C.E.), Japanese architecture embraced influences from the elegant and symmetrical buildings of China's Tang Dynasty, often featuring white plaster walls and dark wooden structures. It could be seen in the Shinden-zukuri estates complex (Illus. 3.1.7). The rise of the samurai class during the Kamakura epoch (1185 C.E.–1333 C.E.) led to the construction of fortifications and castles, reflecting military requirements. The Muromachi era (1336 C.E.–1573 C.E.) introduced architectural details such as tatami-matted rooms and sliding doors (fusuma, Illus. 3.1.8). The Edo Period (1603 C.E.–1868 C.E.) witnessed the growth of the merchant class, influencing the development of machiya townhouses (Illus. 3.1.9) and traditional wooden buildings with latticed windows.

As we can see, Japanese architecture was continually adapting to changing

3.1.4. Shinto Shrine. Japan. 4th century B.C.E. Photo credit: isejingu.or.jp

3.1.5. Horyuji Temple, Nara, Japan. 607 AD. Photo credit: Michael Turtle

3.1.6. Todaiji Temple Nara Park, Japan. 752 CE. Photo credit: Japan Guide

3.1.7. Shinden-zukuri estates.
Photo credit: Anthony J. Bryant

3.1.8. Machiya townhouse. Interior.
Photo credit: Nik van der Giesen

3.1.9. Machiya house. Japan.
Photo credit: Elsa Arribas

needs while retaining its essential principles of simplicity, harmony, and connection with nature. Eventually, metamorphosed by new construction materials and methods, these features of Japanese architecture now play a significant role in contemporary Japanese and world architecture.

IN CHINA, as well as in other neighboring countries, similar climate, material, structural methods, and traditions, along with cultural interrelationships, trade, etc., influenced developments of similar architectural elements, such as courtyards or sweeping roofs with upturned eaves.

During several epochs of China's history, which are named usually after different ruling dynasties (Tang, Song, Ming, and Qing), China's architecture reflected different economic developments. For instance, during the Tang Dynasty (618–907), which marked a prosperous period in Chinese history, its architecture reflected that grandeur. Preserved buildings from this era feature grand halls, pagodas, and multi-story towers. The Bell Tower of Xi'an (Illus. 3.2.1 and 3.2.2) is an excellent example of this epoch. During the Song Dynasty (960–1279) China's architecture witnessed a shift toward more refined elegant buildings. The Ming Dynasty (1368-1644) architecture emphasized grandeur and the use of vibrant colors. The Qing Dynasty (1644-1912) architecture combined elements of previous dynasties but also incorporated influences from Central Asia, as could be seen in the Summer Palace and the Temple of Heaven in Beijing (Illus. 3.2.3).

Analyzing all the changes in architecture brought by these epochs, from one emperor's dynasty to another's, one could notice that the main features of Chinese architecture (symmetrical layouts, sweeping roofs with upturned eaves, and intricate carvings) did not change much from the seventh century up to the twentieth century. Strictly speaking, there were no changes of artistic styles, but the modes: grandeur, vibrant colors, etc.

However, a concept of Chinese traditional architecture, which is known as 'siheyuan' or 'four-sided courtyard' architecture (Illus. 3.2.4 and 3.2.5), and which originally was characterized by wooden structures with bracket sets, known as 'Dougong,' is present throughout the long history of China's architecture. It spans from ancient times, which dates back thousands of years, and up to now. Found in peasant houses as well as in emperors' palaces during the centuries, it produced specific art style features mentioned above, which distinguishes Chinese architecture from others.

In Japanese and Chinese architecture, many art styles changed, but the architecture remained recognizable respectively Japanese or Chinese. The same thing happened in India, Persia, the countries of the Maghreb, and so on.

THE ARCHITECTURE OF INDIA has a rich and diverse history spanning several epochs, each characterized by unique features and influences.[1] Each epoch produced its architecture, which encompasses a wide range of regional influences that have developed over centuries across the diverse regions of the country.

There are distinctive regional variations influenced by climate, geography, culture, and available materials in India.

---

1 Scholars classify Indian history into seven epochs: Indus Valley Civilization (2600 B.C.E.–1900 B.C.E.); Vedic Period (1500 B.C.E.– 00 B.C.E.); Maurya Dynasty (c. 322 B.C.E.–185 B.C.E.); Gupta Dynasty (c. 320 C.E.–550 C.E.); Chola Dynasty (c. 850 C.E.–1250 C.E.); Mughal Empire (1526 C.E.–1857 C.E.); Colonial Era (seventeenth century – mid-twentieth century).

3.2.1. The Bell Tower of Xi'an. Xi'an, China. 1384. Photo by author

3.2.2. The Bell Tower of Xi'an. 1384. Xi'an, China. Photo by author

3.2.3. Temple Of Heaven. Beijing, China. 1420. Photo credit: Travelu.re

For instance, Rajasthani architecture reflects the desert climate of the state of Rajasthan. This architecture is characterized by thick walls, ornate jharokhas (overhanging enclosed balconies), intricate stone carvings, and frescoes (Illus. 3.3.1). Mughal architecture combines Persian, Indian, and Islamic influences. Along with courtyard-based designs, often seen in havelis (traditional Indian townhouses) and the use of chajjas (projecting eaves) to provide shade and ventilation, it features large domes, intricate marble inlays, arches, and beautiful gardens. Dravidian architecture is characterized by temple architecture with pyramid-shaped towers called gopurams, intricate carvings, and vibrant colors. Kerala architecture is influenced by the region's tropical climate and the availability of wood and laterite stone. Kerala houses, known as nalukettu, feature sloping roofs, wooden carvings, open courtyards, and teakwood interiors (Illus. 3.3.2 and 3.3.3). Bengali architecture features curved roofs, intricate terracotta sculptures, and intricate brickwork. Gujarati architecture reflects the region's hot and arid climate and is known for its stepwells (baolis), havelis, and intricately carved wooden houses. Assamese architecture features unique structures such as the traditional bamboo and thatch houses called chang ghars (Illus. 3.3.4, and 3.3.5), along with Assam-type houses made of brick and timber.

These regional architectural features in Indian architecture highlight the diversity and richness of the country's cultural heritage. They reflect the local materials, climate, religious and historical influences, creating a tapestry of architectural traditions across India. However, the totality of all these regional elements such as open courtyard-based designs, intricate brickwork, wooden and stone carvings, marble inlays, beautiful gardens, use of chajjas and ornate jharokhas, all of them together make Indian architecture recognizable and distinguishable as the architecture of Indian continent.

MUSLIM VERNACULAR ARCHITECTURE varied greatly depending on the geographical region and cultural influences. However, generally, it shared some common features. Contemporary scholarship recognizes five main epochs in the development of Muslim vernacular architecture: pre-Islamic, Early Islamic, Medieval, Ottoman, and Mughal. There are also five regional

3.2.4. Reconstruction of a traditional Chinese building in Song Dynasty
Photo credit: Zhu & Zhu

3.2.5. Siheyuan house. China.
Photo credit: Dorothy

3.3.1. Mughal haveli.
Photo credit: Antoine Taveneaux

3.3.2. Gujarati traditional house
Photo credit: Tom Parker

3.3.3. Courtyard in Nalukettu house. Photo credit: Muziris heritage project

3.3.4. Traditional Assamese houses. Photo credit: re-thinkingthefuture.com

3.3.5. Traditional Assamese house. Photo credit: Digangana Medhi

3.4.1. Stone houses, Yemen.
Photo credit: Nevit Dilmen

3.4.2. Traditional Housing. Ghana.
Photo credit: 5-five-5.blogspot.com

3.4.3. UAE. Dubai. Bastakia housing.
Photo credit: Jessica Lee planetware

variations of Muslim vernacular architecture: Maritime Southeast Asia, West African, Central Asian, and Persian.

Before the rise of Islam, various regions had their distinctive architectural traditions. With the spread of Islam, these local forms started to incorporate Islamic elements, such as the use of courtyard layouts and arched doorways (Illus. 3.4.1). During the medieval era, as the Islamic world expanded, numerous local architectural forms emerged such as mud brick (adobe) construction, which became prevalent due to its suitability for the climate and the availability of materials in arid regions like parts of North Africa and the Middle East (Illus. 3.4.2). In hot and arid regions like Iran and parts of the Arabian Peninsula, wind towers (badgirs) were employed to capture and channel cool air into buildings, providing natural ventilation (Illus. 3. 4.3). Ottoman vernacular architecture, which spread across the Balkans, the Middle East, and North Africa, featured the use of timber, stone, and brick. Its distinctive elements include also wooden mashrabiya screens, projecting bay windows, and flat-roofed structures.

In regions like Indonesia and Malaysia, Muslim communities developed their vernacular architecture using organic materials like bamboo, palm thatch, and wood. These structures often featured steeply pitched roofs, raised floors, and open-air living spaces. In East Africa, Muslim communities incorporated Islamic elements into their traditional mud-brick compounds (Illus. 3.4.4 and 3.4.5). These compounds often included enclosed courtyards, decorative patterns, and thatched or flat roofs. In areas like Afghanistan and Central Asia, traditional dwellings included courtyard houses with high walls, wind towers for ventilation, and intricate wooden carvings (Illus. 3.4.6)

Evident in all epochs and regions, the notable aspect of Muslim vernacular architecture, as in any other folk architecture, is its adaptability to local climates, building materials, and cultural practices. Altogether, the common features of Muslim vernacular architecture could be exemplified by courtyard layouts with high walls, arched doorways, wind towers, projecting bay windows, and flat-roofed structures. This architecture reflects the integration of Islamic principles with regional building techniques, resulting in a rich tapestry of diverse architectural forms across the Muslim world.

3.4.4. Egypt housing.
Photo credit: loveproperty.com

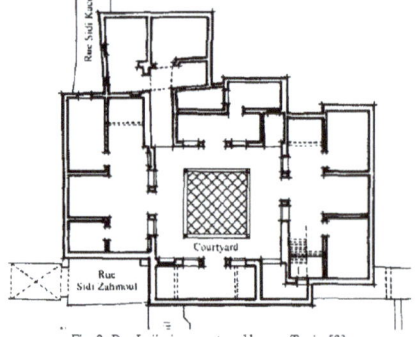

3.4.5. Traditional Islamic-Arab House.
Photo credit: Abdel-moniem El-Shorbagy

3.4.6. Riad House.
Photo credit: Christie's International real estate

ARAB ARCHITECTURE, one of the branches of Muslim architecture, reflects the use of local materials, climate considerations, and cultural practices. It is shaped by the region's hot and dry climate as well as its cultural traditions. Key architectural elements include courtyards, which provide cool and shaded spaces for people to gather and relax, and wind towers, which facilitate ventilation by drawing in cool air from the bottom and releasing hot air from the top. Ornate tilework is also a prominent feature. Traditional Riads houses in Morocco feature inward-facing designs, centered around a courtyard or garden, providing privacy and protection from the desert climate (Illus. 3.5.1). Yemeni architecture is known for its unique tower houses, called "qasabahs" or "rammed-earth skyscrapers" (Illus.3.5.2). These tall structures, which are built with rammed earth, brick, and wood, serve as multi-story dwellings, offering protection from the arid environment and occasional flooding. Windcatchers, also known as "badgirs" or "malqaf," are traditional ventilation systems found in desert regions like Iran, Saudi Arabia, and the United Arab Emirates. They consist of tall, tower-like structures with openings designed to

3.5.1. Houses. Morocco.
Photo credit: kimkim.com

3.5.2. Houses. Yemen.
Photo credit: travelpicturesgallery.com

3.5.3. Arab house with wind tower. Photo credit: Aya Ezz El-Arab

capture and direct cool breezes into buildings, providing natural ventilation and cooling (Illus. 3.5.3 and 3.5.4). In Sudan, mud brick architecture is prevalent due to the availability of local materials. The buildings are constructed using mud bricks and are often characterized by domed roofs, arched doorways, and decorative patterns etched into the walls. Found in countries like Kuwait, Bahrain, and Qatar, barajeel houses are traditional homes designed to maximize natural ventilation (Illus. 3.5.5 and 3.5.6). They have wind towers (barajeel) on the rooftops that catch the prevailing winds and direct them into the interior spaces, providing natural cooling.

Whatever we find and cherish as a distinctive representation of national architecture is the result of the centuries-long solution's search for folk's architecture everyday tasks. Describing the Central Asian branch of Muslim architecture, Moisei Ginzburg wrote that "in this labyrinth of crooked and narrow streets knocked off their axes, in the asymmetry and transverse length of individual parts and courtyards, in the clarity of the volumes of this primitive architecture, in flat roofs and in the original interpretation of the wall surface,

3.5.4. House. Al-Ula, Saudi Arabia. Photo cfedit: Hisham Mortada

3.5.5. Wind tower. UAE. Photo credit: beautifulinterior1.blogspot.com

3.5.6. Wind tower. Dubai. Photo credit: smccudubai.wordpress.com

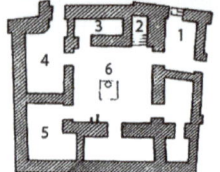

1-Entrance
2-Staircase
3-Washroom
4-Kitchen
5-Storeroom
6-Courtyard

3.6.1. Reed house reconstruction.
Photo credit: Qassim Said and Al-Dawoud

3.7.1. Egypt mud brick housing
Photo credit: flicr.com

where the opening of a window or door is drowned in the ascetic whiteness of the flat surfaces—all this is reflected in the many functional prerequisites of the East, which forged this peculiar look."[2]

In Western civilization, architecture went through several epochs too: Mesopotamia, Ancient Egypt, Greece, and Rome, Medieval times, and Renaissance.

THE HISTORY OF MESOPOTAMIA spans several epochs, and each epoch had its impact on vernacular architecture. Prehistoric Mesopotamia (circa 10,000–3500 B.C.E.) dwellings were usually rectangular or circular and served as basic shelters for the community. Sumerian Civilization (circa 3500–2340 B.C.E. houses were made of mud-brick and reed (Illus. 3.6.1). Akkadian and Babylonian Periods (circa 2340–1595 B.C.E.) contributed to the growth of monumental architecture, including larger palaces, temples, and city walls. Assyrian Civilization (circa 1900–612 B.C.E.) made advancements in military fortifications. The use of baked bricks became more prevalent during this period. Throughout these epochs, mud-brick and baked brick

---

[2] Ginzburg, Moisei. "Tvorcheskiye puti Sovietskoi arkhitektury (Creative way of the Soviet Architecture.)" Journal Arkhitektura SSSR (Architecture of the USSR). Moscow, USSR. 1933, No 3-4.

3.7.2. Ancient Egypt mud brick houses. Photo credit: Pinterest

were the primary building materials due to the abundance of clay in the region. These materials were cheap and easy to work with, but they required regular maintenance, especially in the face of the annual flooding of the rivers. Vernacular architecture in Mesopotamia was deeply connected to the geography, climate, and available resources, and it has influenced the region's culture and architecture for millennia.

ANCIENT EGYPTIAN vernacular architecture went through several epochs, from the Predynastic Period (circa 3000–2650 B.C.E.) to the Late Period and Ptolemaic Period (664–30 B.C.E.). Throughout these epochs, the basic principles of Ancient Egyptian vernacular architecture remained relatively consistent, centered around using local materials like mud bricks and reeds, and adapting designs to the hot and arid climate of Egypt (Illus. 3.7.1 and 3.7.2). Typology of ancient Egyptian vernacular architecture developed from rectangular-shaped mudbrick houses with courtyards and defined rooms to more complex layouts, featuring multiple rooms and sometimes multiple stories.

THE EPOCHS OF ANCIENT GREECE vernacular architecture span from the Early Greek Period (ca. 900-

700 B.C.E.) through its Hellenistic Period (ca. 323–31 B.C.E.). During this time, Ancient Greek vernacular architecture underwent significant development, from mud-brick houses with thatched roofs to stone and timber rectangular houses with one or more rooms around a central courtyard. The specific characteristics of Ancient Greece's vernacular architecture varied from region to region, as different city-states had their distinct building traditions and practices.

ANCIENT ROME'S vernacular architecture evolved over several centuries, and it can be divided into several main epochs, each characterized by different influences.

During the Pre-Roman and Early Roman Period (before 509 B.C.E.), the buildings were simple huts and houses made from local materials like wood, thatch, and mud. The Roman Republic's (509 B.C.E.–27 B.C.E.) vernacular architecture consisted of basic stone and clay brick buildings with a focus on functionality. These structures often had atriums and were centered around family life. During the Early Imperial Period (27 B.C.E.–2nd century C.E.) Roman engineers and architects developed construction techniques using concrete, which allowed them to create larger and more durable structures. Vernacular buildings of this time included apartment buildings, shops, and warehouses, along with grand villas in the countryside (Illus. 3.8.1). The High Imperial Period (2nd century C.E.–3rd century C.E.) witnessed the peak of Roman power and prosperity, leading to the construction of monumental structures like the Colosseum and the Pantheon. However, the vernacular architecture for ordinary citizens continued to focus on practicality and functionality, with more standardized construction techniques. The Late Antique Period (3rd century C.E.– 5th century C.E.) saw significant changes due to economic decline and political instability. The construction of private homes became more modest, often featuring basilica-like designs.

Ancient Roman vernacular architecture was influenced by various additional factors, such as social class, available resources, and the evolution of construction techniques.

Due to the necessity of building public and religious buildings, Ancient Greece developed the post-and-beam system of their vernacular architecture. Long before the Greeks this system

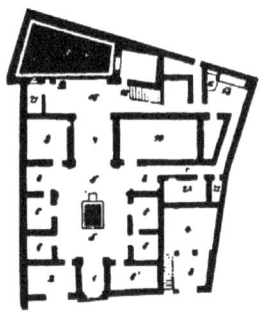

3.8.1. Roman houses. Photo credit: Vitruvius. The Ten Books on Architecture. Book 6, Ch 3. p. 176

was accepted by the ancient Egyptians too. Greeks developed it into a high art of construction. Ancient Rome supplemented the system with the art of constructing arches. In both cases, the age-old experience of architecture gradually resulted in a coherent system of architectural orders. Due to the death of the Greek and Roman civilizations, this system was forgotten for many centuries. Later on, European architecture went through several eras until it was divided into the architectures of the states formed in Europe, and came back to use these orders during the Renaissance era, however as a matter of decoration.

GERMAN national architecture reflects a diverse range of cultural and historical influences across different regions of Germany. It embodies the local materials, climatic conditions, and traditional building techniques unique to each area. German architecture is often characterized by fachwerk structures, which consist of timber-framed constructions filled with brick, stone, or plaster panels. Over time, distinctive regional variations of German architecture have emerged. The Hallenhaus-type buildings, typical in southern Germany, are rectangular structures with a central corridor running the length of the house. The Uthlandfriesisches Haus, found in the coastal regions of Northern Germany, is known for its spacious open living areas and distinctive gables. German medieval housing is known for its distinctive brick or brick and timber-framed walls (Illus. 3.9.1).

ENGLISH national architecture also encompasses a wide range of building types that have developed in different parts of England throughout history. It showcases the local materials, building techniques, and historical contexts, resulting in a rich tapestry of architectural heritage across the country. Notable English regional variations include among others Tudor (Illus. 3.10.1), Costwold (Illus. 3.10.2), and Yorkshire (Illus. 3.10.3) architecture. These variations often feature timber-framed or limestone structures, mullioned windows, prominent chimneys, and steeply pitched roofs.

UKRAINIAN vernacular architecture, which has evolved over centuries is closely tied to the local climate, landscape, and cultural practices. While there is diversity in it due to regional variations, some common features can be identified, such as the use of wood,

3.9.1. German House. Photo credit: kweinland

3.10.1. Tudor House in England. Photo credit: Gerd Eichmann

3.10.2. Costwood houses, England. Photo credit: Tobias Vogt von Heselholt

3.10.3. Yorkshire house. Photo credit: houzz.com

3.11.1. Ukrainian House. Photo credit: Andrii, Wiki Ukrainian

thatched and large sloping roofs with overhanging eaves in the Carpathian region, and intricate woodwork (Illus. 3.11.1).

Traditional Ukrainian cottages often have simple rectangular or square shape open floor plans with all activities arranged around centrally located stoves, a gabled roof, and whitewashed walls with decorative wooden elements in the Poltava region (Illus. 3.11.2). In the Podillia region residential architecture is influenced by the local landscape, with houses built into hillsides.

3.11.2. Ukrainian house. XI century. Photo credit: Uk-Kamelot, Wikimedia

RUSSIAN vernacular architecture has developed in different regions of Russia over time. It is also influenced by the climate, geography, available materials, and cultural practices of the specific area. It reflects a wide range of climates, from cold continental climates to more temperate zones by incorporating features such as steep roofs to shed snow, thick walls for insulation, and small windows to conserve heat.

In northern regions, where wood is abundant, log construction is common. In areas with more access to stone, such as the Caucasus region, stone may be used for construction. Adobe and brick are also used in some regions. Wooden architecture is prevalent in many parts of Russia. Traditional wooden houses are often characterized by their log construction, with dovetail joints and intricate wooden carvings.

A traditional Russian log house, called *izba*, is typically one or one and a half stories high, with a steep thatched or shingled roof. Isbas often have a rectangular plan with a central hearth for heating and food preparation. Traditional Russian architecture often includes elaborate decorative elements.

In the Siberia region, which is known for its harsh climate, one could

3.12.1. Wooden house. Tomsk. Russia. Photo credit: Adam Jones, Wikimedia

find log houses with elaborate wooden carvings, painted motifs, and ornate window frames (Illus. 3.12.1), reflecting Chinese art influence. Siberian homes often include multi-functional spaces, with one area serving as a living space, sleeping quarters, and sometimes even as a storage area. Roofs are typically steeply pitched to allow snow to slide off easily and prevent the accumulation of heavy snow loads.

Similar developments could be noticed in other continents also.

MEXICAN ARCHITECTURE, for instance, is incredibly diverse, reflecting the country's rich history and cultural influences, including indigenous Mesoamerican, Spanish colonial, and contemporary design elements (Illus. 3.13.1 and 3.13.2). Adapted to the local climate and traditions, Mexican architecture often incorporates features such as heat-resistant thick walls, vibrant colors, intricate ornamentation, and the use of local materials.

3.13.2. Mexican House.
Photo credit: Pintrest

3.13.1. Mexican Adobe house. 1904. Photo credit: postcard

3.14.1. American shotgun house. New Orleans, Louisiana. USA. Photo credit: Sarah Magnuson

THE UNITED STATES, another relatively young country, has likewise a diverse architectural landscape that also reflects its climate, history, traditions, and culture. American architecture often emphasizes natural light, incorporates wood and regional materials, promotes harmony with nature, and showcases the influence of various cultures (Illus. 3.14.1, 3.14.2 and 3.14.3). The term 'American Architecture' is often associated specifically with U.S. skyscrapers architecture. However, a more accurate representation would encompass a broader array of U.S. architectural trends, such as Cape Cod, Georgian, Prairie School, Victorian, Contemporary, and others.

ANCIENT ISRAEL architecture encompasses a vast period, ranging from the Bronze Age to the Roman period, and it evolved significantly over this period. However, it's important to recognize that our knowledge of vernacular architecture in ancient Israel comes from archaeological findings, historical texts, and other sources, which are scarce and there may still be gaps and uncertainties in our understanding

3.14.2. American log cabin house. Photo credit: houzz.com

3.14.3. Pueblo House. New Mexico. USA. Photo credit: TerraGalleria

of specific details. Since ancient Israel's architecture was destroyed by Romans, and information about it is limited, we could only guess that its architecture was developing along the lines of other Mediterranean nations' architecture. It does not help that most ancient Israelites were nomads, and therefore, they did not have too many settlements. However, there is evidence to suggest the presence of Hebrew-speaking Jewish communities in certain regions of ancient Europe. These communities started to spread to different parts of the world after the Babylonian exile in the sixth century B.C.E. and continued to migrate and settle in various regions throughout history. The Danube River served as an important trade route and migration corridor, attracting various communities, including Jewish populations. Jewish settlements along the Danube River in Europe (present-day Bulgaria, Ukraine, Romania, Hungary, Czechia, Austria, and Germany) have a long and varied history, dating back to ancient times. During the Roman and Byzantine periods, there were Jewish communities established in other parts of Europe, including Italy, Greece, and the Iberian Peninsula. Later in history, these communities became a part of the worldwide Jewish diaspora. We could guess that the ancient architecture of the settlements, where these communities resided, was, probably, reflecting their social structure, local climate, available materials, and methods of construction.

Most likely, ancient architecture in Israel proper included, similar to their neighbors' dwellings, single-story courtyard-type houses with flat roofs, ventilation towers, and walled neighborhoods. In the coastal areas, stone and clay bricks were common, probably, while in the inland regions, where stone was scarce, mud bricks and other elements, which we can find in neighboring countries' architecture were more prevalent. The main religious structure was the Temple in Jerusalem, which underwent various reconstructions over time before it was demolished by the Romans. Unlike other nations' architecture, Israel's did not have a chance to develop. It was abruptly ended by the Romans in the first century of C.E.

The descriptions of mentioned above different countries' and regions' architecture clearly illustrate a well-known fact: the architectural face of each nation is created by the totality of specific national stylistic architectural forms and details, which were developed by traditional vernacular architecture, and have been influenced by climate, construction materials and methods, traditions, and the aesthetic preferences of the people inhabiting a specific land. This is why one could easily distinguish, say, German architecture from Japanese or, for example, Mexican, and Arabic from Chinese, Indian or American, and so on.

Since Jewish national architecture did not continue to exist after the Jewish nation was dispersed by the Romans and formed a Jewish diaspora around the globe, the Jews were involved in construction activities on other nation's lands. Did they produce distinctive, at least—conditionally, Jewish Architecture in the structures they built in host countries? This is the subject of our study in the next chapter.

Chapter 4. Jewish Structures in the Host Countries

Our previous chapters were devoted to outlining the subject of architecture as a human endeavor aimed at creating habitat, exploring architecture's elements, and the exemplification of national architecture's features relevant to our task of defining *Jewish Architecture*. The Jewish nation in diaspora was involved in building activities, however on the host countries' territories. To find out if these activities produced *Jewish Architec-ture*, we shall investigate whether Jewish input into these nations' architectures could be viewed as such. And indeed, can Jewish buildings like housing, syna-gogues, cemetery structures, etc. erected on the territory of host countries be considered *Jewish Architecture*? In short, are Jewish buildings the *Jewish Architec-ture*?

Since the essence of any national architecture could be found in its housing, let us see first, if we could find *Jewish Architecture* in the Jewish houses built in the host countries.

There is no information on Jewish dwellings in ancient Egypt, Greece, Rome, or Israel. Remains of Jewish vernacular architecture can be found in medieval structures of Central Asia, the Middle East, the Far East, and Europe.

JEWISH DWELLINGS IN CENTRAL ASIA. This region was a significant hub along the Silk Road and encompasses a vast area with diverse cultures and architectural traditions. The vernacular architecture of Central Asia reflects the unique environmen-tal conditions, nomadic lifestyle, and cultural influences around the territo-ry. Jews from Central Asia are mainly Bukharian Jews, who historically lived in the Emirate of Bukhara (present-day Uzbekistan and Tajikistan). They are claiming descent from fifth-century exiles from Persia, and have resisted several waves of persecution and assimi-lation through the development of their own distinct Jewish culture. However, their housing architecture followed local customs and traditions. The houses of Bukharian Jews (Illus.4.1.1) represent exceptional living examples of vernacular architecture within a medieval urban design and a Muslim community's system of mahallahs, or neighborhoods. Their houses, known as 'havtiq,' typically have a central courtyard, which serves as communal spaces for families and religious gatherings, high walls, and rooms arranged around the perimeter. They adapt to the extreme temperatures and climatic conditions. Buildings have thick walls for insulation, small windows to reduce direct sunlight, and other features that help maintain a comfortable indoor environment. Traditional building materials of Central Asia, such as adobe or mud bricks, are commonly used in Jewish vernacular architecture.

These materials are well-suited for the arid climate of the region.

JEWISH DWELLINGS IN EGYPT. The Jewish Quarter in Alexandria may serve as an example of Jewish dwellings in Egypt (Illus.4.2.1). It is a historic neighborhood that was once home to a large and thriving Jewish community. The neighborhood is characterized by its narrow streets, traditional houses, and synagogues, reflecting the customs and traditions of local Muslim architecture. As a typical example of a medieval Jewish dwelling, there is a small, two-story mudbrick house in Fustat (old Cairo), featuring a central courtyard, a kitchen with a brick oven,

4.1.1. Jewish house in Bukhara. Central Asia. Photo credit: public domain

4.2.1. Jewish quarter in Alexandria, Egypt. 1898. Photo credit: Ashashyou

and separate living quarters for men and women (Illus.4.2.2).

JEWISH DWELLINGS IN MOROCCO. The Mellah of Fes in Morocco is one of the oldest and largest Jewish quarters in the world, dating back to the fourteenth century. It is a labyrinthine network of narrow streets, enclosed by a wall. The houses are typically built around a central courtyard, with balconies overlooking the street. Established in the sixteenth century, Mellah of Marrakesh (Illus. 4.3.1) still retains some medieval features. The houses are constructed with traditional materials like rammed earth and wood, and many have internal courtyards. Jewish houses in the Casbah of Essaouira are built in the traditional Moroccan architecture, with courtyards and balconies. By comparing medieval Jewish dwellings in Morocco, which are indistinguishable from those of their non-Jewish neighbors, one can gain a better understanding of the local influences that shaped their architecture.

JEWISH DWELLINGS IN TUNIS. Examples of Jewish houses in Tunis include the Djerba Erriadh, house (Illus. 4.4.1). It was built in the eighteenth century and is considered to be one of the best-preserved examples of a tradi-tional Jewish house in the city. Follow-ing local architectural traditions and

4.2.2. Egyptian mud brick houses. Photo credit: animalia-life.club

4.3.1. Jewish homes in Marrakech, Morocco. Photo credit: Michal Shmulovich

customs, Jewish houses in Tunis featured usually a central courtyard, which served as a gathering space for the family and a place to relax and escape the heat. Arranged around this courtyard were typically four or five rooms. The rooms included a living room, a kitchen, a bedroom, a study, and a storage room. Some houses also had balconies overlooking the courtyard or the street. The balconies were often made of wood and decorated with intricate latticework. The walls of a Jewish house were typically made of mudbrick or stone and were often painted white or a light color, and they might have been decorated with geometric patterns or calligraphic inscriptions. And, again, they are indistinguishable from their Muslim neighbor's houses.

JEWISH DWELLINGS IN GERMANY. The Rhineland in Germany is the area where the Jews started to settle during the time of the Roman Empire. The Jewish quarters in Trier represent one of the best surviving examples of Jewish housing in Germany (Illus. 4.5.1). Also, it is the oldest Jewish house in the country. Featuring a distinctive half-timber facade, it boasts multiple rooms likely designated for both residential and commercial use. It stands out as one of the most renowned and best-preserved examples of a medieval Jewish dwelling in Germany. The house

4.4.1. Jewish house in Djerba Erriadh, Tunis. Photo credit: Pinterest

4.5.1. The oldest Jewish House in Trier, Germany. Photo credit: sedulia.blogs.com

shows how Jewish dwelling architecture followed the main tenets of the German habitat of the time.

JEWISH DWELLINGS IN ENGLAND. One of the well-known examples of Jewish houses in England is the Jew's House in Lincoln (Illus.4.6.1). The house is named after Bellaset of Wallingford, a Jewish woman who owned it in the late 13th century, and was tragically executed in 1287 for the false accusation of clipping coins. It is a famous medieval Jewish stone residence, which is considered the oldest occupied house in Europe, dating back to the mid-12th century. It is a two-story structure made of limestone. The building is a typical representative of this region's medieval English architecture.

JEWISH DWELLINGS IN UKRAINE. Like those in many other parts of the world, Jewish homes in Ukraine vary based on location, socioeconomic status, and individual preferences. While the interiors of these dwellings may share general traditions common to Jewish homes worldwide, their specific features reflect the local Ukrainian context. These features can be influenced by factors such as the region and historical experiences (Illus. 4.7.1). However, observant Jewish households may maintain a kosher kitchen. It could be a designated space in the house for

4.6.1. Jew's House, Lincoln, England. Photo credit: Richard Croft geograph.org.uk

4.7.1. Old Jewish house. Verkhnyaya Bystra. Ukraine. Photo credit: Karin Wandrei

Shabbat (Sabbath) observance. Some Jewish families may have a designated area for daily prayers or the study of religious texts. Many Jewish homes in Ukraine may have a strong emphasis on learning. This could manifest in a home library, educational materials, or a space dedicated to study. Spaces for family gatherings, celebrations, and meals may be prioritized. Usually, a mezuzah is affixed to the doorpost. Otherwise, Jewish dwellings are impossible to distinguish from the homes of their non-Jewish neighbors.

JEWISH DWELLINGS IN RUSSIA. They reflect a blend of Jewish cultural traditions and the architectural trends prevalent in the regions where Jewish communities have historically resided (Illus. 4.8.1). However, it's crucial to note that Jewish houses in Russia, as in other parts of the world, are diverse and can vary significantly based on factors such as location, historical period, and individual circumstances. Usually located in rural settings, they are part of small villages or towns and merge with the neighboring buildings (Illus. 4.8.2). Some traditional Jewish homes, especially in the eastern part of the country, had a central courtyard, providing privacy and serving as a focal point for family activities. During the festival of Sukkot, temporary structures called sukkahs were constructed.

The same pattern in vernacular architecture exists in other host countries. As we have seen, quite expectantly, Jewish dwellings in the countries of exile re-semble residential buildings of the local population. There was no specific *Jewish Architecture* in them. But what about *Jewish Architecture* in the synagogue buildings?

Preserved religious buildings are among the most surviving architectural artifacts. As we shall see, while the buildings of temples, churches, and mosques represented their respective nations, the buildings of the synagogues demonstrated the current cultural traditions of the host nations similarly to the residential architecture. Synagogues in all host countries contain features of the national architecture of these nations. It could be seen by comparing several religious buildings of different nations: a Japanese or Chinese temple, an Arab mosque, a Catholic church, and a synagogue.

In Europe, building synagogues was one of the most important parts

4.8.1. Old Jewish House, Kazan, Russia. Photo credit: Tata Gudlin

of Jewish architectural activity on the host country land before Jewish emancipation. From the Middle Ages onwards typology of synagogues and their buildings became more and more sophisticated, responding to communities' needs and aspirations. They went from the simple single nave of wooden synagogues to nine-nave ma-sonry structures with side galleries and elaborate decorations. The latter trend was developing sometimes against the aspirations of common Jews. As Carol Herselle Krinsky noticed, "Most synagogues in Eastern Europe were simple rooms with modest furnishings, though often loved by their congregations as if they were their own homes. Adherents of the ultra-orthodox, mystically-orient-ed Hasidim sect, which was prominent, especially in Eastern Europe, from the late eighteenth century onward, professed indifference to their surroundings during prayer and devoted more attention to rooms where they studied. Karaites, a small minority of Jews who do not follow the Talmud, the record of orally transmitted Jewish law, also had modest synagogues. These were especially simple rooms because they dispensed with the furnishings associated with Talmudic study and requirements. Deeply pious traditional Jews often echoed Talmudic authorities who asked why the money used for handsome synagogues had not been used instead to support studies of the Torah, which is Jewish law in its widest sense."[1] Existing scholarship on this subject sometimes classifies synagogue buildings by certain 'art styles': Egyptian, Romanesque, Byzantine, Rundbogenstill, Moorish-Islamic,

---

[1] Krinsky, Carol Herselle. *Synagogues of Europe: Architecture, History, Meaning.* The MIT Press, Cambridge, MA. 1985. P. 3

Gothic, Late-nine-teenth-century, Early-twentieth-century, and so on. However, in our analysis, we will group synagogues by the host countries of Jews.

SYNAGOGUES IN JAPAN. One of the first synagogues in Japan was built in Nagasaki in 1894 (Illus. 4.9.1). It was a small building that was used by a small community of Jewish immigrants from Europe. A second synagogue was built in Kobe. This synagogue was larger and more ornate than the first one, and it became the center of the Jewish community in Japan. Specific Japanese features of synagogues in Japan include the use of natural materials such as wood and stone, which is in keeping with Japanese architectural traditions. Often incorporated into the design of synagogues are Japanese gardens. These gardens may contain Japanese motifs such as cherry blossoms, bamboo, and koi fish as a way to connect the building to Japanese culture.

SYNAGOGUES IN CHINA. The presence of Jews in China can be traced back to ancient times, although the exact date of their arrival is not well-documented. Historical evidence suggests that Jewish traders and settlers may have arrived in China as early as the Tang Dynasty (618–907 C.E.) or even earlier during the Han Dynasty (202 B.C.E.–220 C.E.). There are no remains of synagogues from these early times. Judging by the Chinese written artifacts, archaeologists assume that the oldest synagogues in China were built in the 8th century. Most likely they were modeled after Chinese temples. One of the sources for this is information about the Kaifeng synagogue. The Kaifeng Jews were one notable group of Jews in China. They are believed to have settled in the city of Kaifeng during the Song Dynasty (960–1279 C.E.). The Kaifeng Jew-ish community flourished for several centuries, and they built a synagogue in the city, which was completed in the seventeenth century (Illus.4.10.1 and 4.10.2). This synagogue is a fine example of the fusion of Chinese and Jewish cultures. The exterior of the synagogue has a pagoda-style roof and a courtyard. The interior of the synagogue has a central hall with a raised platform at the front, where the Torah scrolls were kept. The walls were decorated with Jewish symbols and motifs as well as with Chinese paintings and calligraphy.

4.9.1. Beth Israel Synagogue, Nagasaki, Japan. 1894. Photo credit: public domain

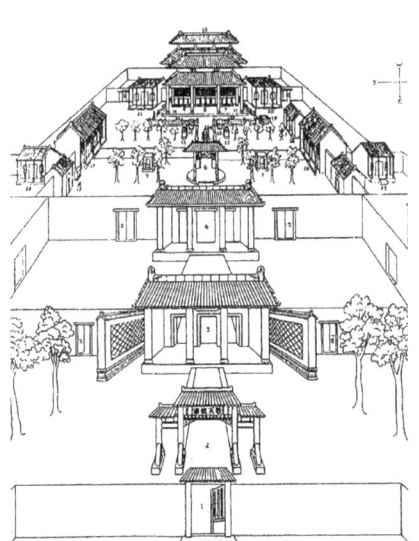

4.10.1. Synagogue. Kaifeng, China. 1163. Interior. Photo credit: myjewishlearning.com

4.10.2. Synagogue. Kaifeng, China. 1163. Interior. Photo credit: myjewishlearning.com

One of the most distinctive features of synagogue architecture in China is the use of the courtyard. The courtyard is a traditional Chinese architectural element, and it is used in synagogues to create a sense of peace and tranquility. The courtyard is also used to separate the synagogue from the outside world, and it provides a place for people to gather before and after services. Besides courtyards, among other distinctive features of synagogue architecture in China are the use of Pagoda-style roofs, and Chinese paintings and calligraphy. The roof of a synagogue is typically made of tiles. It provides shade and protection from the elements, and it is often decorated with Chinese and Jewish symbols.

SYNAGOGUES IN INDIA. The Jewish presence in India has a long and diverse history, dating back over 2,000 years. It is believed that Jewish communities arrived in India during ancient times, possibly as early as the first millennium B.C.E. The earliest surviving synagogues in India were built in the sixteenth century by the Bene Israel community. These synagogues were modeled after local Hindu homes. With the arrival of Jews from Portugal in the sixteenth century, some of the synagogues were modeled after Portuguese churches. These synagogues had a central hall with a raised platform at the front, where the Torah scrolls were kept. In the seventeenth century, a new era of synagogue architecture emerged in India, influenced by the arrival of the Baghdadi Jewish community. These synagogues were larger and more ornate than the earlier synagogues. The central hall was surrounded by smaller rooms, and the walls were decorated with Jewish symbols and motifs.

The most famous Indian synagogues are the synagogue in the town of Paravur in Kerala (Illus.4.11.1 and 4.11.2); the synagogue in the town of Kalyan in Maharashtra (eighteenth century); the synagogue in the city of Chennai in Tamil Nadu (seventeenth century); the synagogue in the suburb of Bandra in Mumbai (nineteenth century). The largest synagogue in India is the Magen David Synagogue in Mumbai, which was built in 1864. This synagogue is a fine example of the fusion of Jewish and Indian architectural elements. The exterior of the synagogue has a dome and a portico. The interior of the synagogue has a central hall, a raised platform, and walls decorated with Jewish symbols and motifs. The main features of Indian

4.11.1. The Paravur synagogue. Kerala, India. 12th century. Photo credit: Muziris Heritage

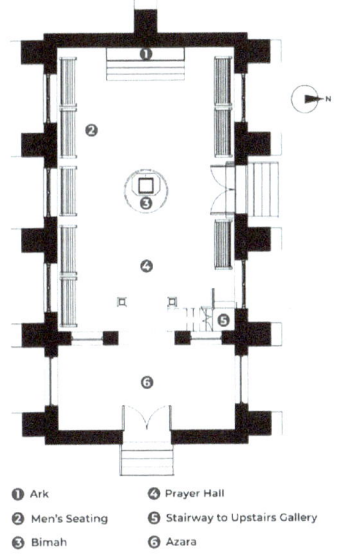

1. Ark
2. Men's Seating
3. Bimah
4. Prayer Hall
5. Stairway to Upstairs Gallery
6. Azara

4.11.2. Typical floor plan of a synagogue. Kerala, India. Photo credit: Robin Thomas

4.12.1. Synagogue. Worms, Germany. 11th century. Photo credit: public domain

synagogues include a central hall, raised platform, pyramidal roofs, domes, porticos, pillars, and courtyards.

SYNAGOGUES IN GERMANY. The oldest synagogue in Germany and one of the oldest surviving synagogues in the world is in the town of Worms (Illus. 4.12.1). This synagogue is a two-story building, with a central hall on the ground floor and a women's gallery on the second floor. Another one is the Esslingen am Neckar Synagogue (Illus. 4.12.2). It is a three-story build-

4.12.2. Synagogue. Esslingen am Neckar, Germany. 1817.
Photo credit: Wikimedia Commons

4.12.3. Synagogue. Blomberg, Germany. 1808. Photo credit: Grugerio [CC BY-SA 3.0 de] Wikimedia Commons

ing, with a central hall on the ground floor and two women's galleries on the second and third floors. The Blomberg synagogue also has a central hall on the ground floor and a second-floor women's gallery, however, on one side only (Illus.4.12.3). German synagogues often incorporate traditional local building elements, such as stone construction and half-timbering.

SYNAGOGUES IN POLAND.

This country was home to a vibrant Jewish community, and synagogues played a central role in the religious and communal life of the Jewish population. The architectural features of Polish synagogues before Jewish emancipation reflected both local influences and the broader trends in Jewish synagogue design. Many synagogues in Poland during this period were constructed using wood, a common building material in the region (Illus. 4.13.1). Wooden synagogues often had intricately designed vaulted ceilings, displaying geometric patterns or representations of the cosmos. In urban centers and wealthier communities, some synagogues were built using masonry. Some masonry synagogues featured domed roofs, contributing to the overall grandeur of the structure. The central elevated platform or bimah, from which the Torah was read, was a prominent feature. It was often positioned in the center of the synagogue. In some cases, synagogues also served as community centers, with adjacent rooms used for meetings, communal gatherings, or educational purposes.

Built in the early seventeenth century, the Zniadowo Synagogue (Illus.4.13.2) was one of the most beautiful wooden synagogues in Poland. It comprised of a central chamber featuring an octagonal vaulted ceiling

4.13.1. Polish wooden synagogue. Photo credit: virtual shtetl web site.

4.13.2. Synagogue. Śniadowo. Poland. 1768.
Photo credit: Konrad Kadush, Israel National Library

upheld by four columns, bordered by corner pavilions of two stories each, topped with pyramidal roofs. It had a unique multi-domed roof and intricate interior decorations. Unfortunately, it did not survive World War II. Among notable Polish synagogues was the Zabudlow synagogue (Illus. 4.13.3). It was known for its unique architecture, and featured a three-domed roof. It was also destroyed during World War II.

SYNAGOGUES IN RUSSIA. In the Russian Empire, Jews were allowed to live only in the Pale of Settlement, which encompasses approximately current Ukraine, and in Siberia, where they ended up either as former Russian soldiers or as prisoners of war with Poland. Russian Siberian vernacular architecture including synagogues incorporates usually traditional Chinese architectural elements, such as elaborate wooden carvings, turrets, and onion-shaped roofs. The best example of it is the synagogue in Tomsk (Illus. 4.14.1).

SYNAGOGUES IN UKRAINE. Some of the most notable synagogues in Ukraine are the Golden Rose Synagogue in Lviv, which was built in 1582; the Zolochiv Synagogue, which was built in 1630; the Choral Synagogue of Bila Tserkva (Illus. 4.15.1), which was built in 1860. A similar wooden synagogue was constructed in Felstztyn (Illus. 4.15.2). Traditionally, synagogues in the Pale of Settlement in Russia were quite modest.[2] Sometimes, the synagogues, made of wood, might be very hard to distinguish from neighboring homes.[3] Rooms for worship often were no more than 150–200 square feet in size, with their domes, if any, concealed in the attic. The interiors were quite in accord with the standards of the time and place.[4] In the Middle Ages especially, comparable synagogues had been built in the West. Ukrainian synagogues often incorporate traditional Ukrainian architectural elements, such as domes, turrets, and onion-shaped roofs.

---

2 See: Kotlyar, E. *Sinagogi yevreiskikh mestechek (Jewish Village Synagogues)*, http://www.judaica.kiev.ua/Eg_14/14-20.htm. [In Russian]. Also: http://www.yivoencyclopedia.org/article.aspx/Synagogue_Architecture

3 See: *100 yevreiskikh mestechek Ukrainy (100 Jewish Villages of the Ukraine)*. Issue 1: Podoliya. Jerusalem-St.-St. Petersburg, 1997, p. 52. [In Russian].

4 See: EYE; http://www.eleven.co.il/article/13810 [In Russian].

4.13.3. Wooden Synagogue. Zabudlow, Poland. 1930s. Photo credit: public domain

4.14.1. The Soldiers Synagogue. Tomsk, Russia. Photo credit: Chaan Liphshiz.

4.15.1. Wooden Synagogue. Bila Tserkva, Ukraine. Photo credit: public domain

4.15.2. Wooden Synagogue. Felsztyn (now Skelivka), Ukraine. Photo credit: public domain

SYNAGOGUE BUILDINGS IN ARAB COUNTRIES are influenced by mosques' architecture. The Great Synagogue of Aleppo (Illus. 4.16.1), constructed in the 5th century C.E., was the Middle East's largest and most esteemed synagogue. Its main courtyard includes a raised pulpit, a yeshivah study hall above, and a chamber in the roof eaves served as a genizah for old reli-gious documents. The western hall has three Torah scroll arks, while the south-ern wall has three more. The Lazama Synagogue in Marrakesh, Morocco, has a highly decorated courtyard, a typical feature of the local vernacular architecture (Illus. 4.16.2).

Similar synagogue buildings could be seen in Babylonia, the Holy Land, Spain, and the Maghreb, where it was customary to use adjacent courtyards as an open-air synagogue in the summer-time. Early Christian churches copied synagogues. The bimah, the ark of the scrolls, the mikveh, and the scroll table in the synagogues were used in the churches respectively as the pulpit, apse, baptistery, and supper table of the Lord. For centuries, synagogue layout, mainly, did not change. However, in the early nineteenth century, a reformist religious movement was born among emancipated Jews. Changes were made to the reli-gious service, which began to resemble a Christian one, and the synagogues of the reformers began to resemble churches more and more. It could be seen in a three-nave layout typical for churches, now used in the synagogues; an organ and a choir appeared in the synagogues. The Bimah was moved from the center of a synagogue to the Ark. Stained glass windows appeared. The gender division was removed. Sermons were delivered now in German, Italian, Polish, and so on, rather than in Hebrew.

To summarize, while creating their physical environment among other na-tions, Jews built in various climatic and social conditions, and their structures imitated, in one way or another, archi-tectural trends of the local population's buildings. Dispersed around the globe, Jews did not produce architecture with specific Jewish national flavor, which we could call *Jewish Architecture*, like we see, say, in Moslem, Chinese, or Japanese buildings.[5] Not surprisingly, at

---

[5] Partially, because all of their buildings were constructed on someone's territory and were necessarily temporary: Jews were always strangers in foreign lands, and, at a certain point, no longer welcome. As a rule, they did not possess the land on which they created real estate.

4.16.1. Synagogue. Aleppo, Syria. Photo credit: Govorkov cc-by-2.0.

4.16.2. The Lazama Synagogue. Marrakesh, Morocco. Photo credit: Michal Shmulovich.

the 2004–2006 international exhibit, Jewish Identity in Contemporary Architecture, which featured contemporary buildings associated with Jewish history and culture, Jewish Architecture was not perceived as the identifying mark of a particularly Jewish quality in architecture. Buildings featured in this exhibition (several museums dedicated to the Holocaust, synagogues, Jewish museums, and schools) were presented as just a part of Jewish heritage. For almost 2,000 years of the Diaspora, the Jews didn't have a Jewish state where they could develop their architecture. Therefore, it is impossible to find traces of genuine *Jewish Architecture* in the ruins of European ghettos or the little that remains of the shtetls in Poland, within the Pale of Settlement in the western region of the former Imperial Russia, or the former Jewish districts of German towns. This included houses and synagogues, which were usually indistinguishable from local peasant dwellings.

As we saw, starting from ancient times to the 1800s, meaning—before emancipation, Jewish structures were influenced by local architecture. However, following the attainment of equal rights during the nineteenth century, Jews gained the ability to influence the architecture of host nations. Their impact was so significant that it completely altered the trajectory of architecture during the twentieth century. This will be the focus of the upcoming chapters.

Chapter 5. Precursors of Global Architecture

In previous chapters, we delved into a range of Jewish Architecture-relat-ed topics, including architecture's fundamental components and the defining features of national architecture. We also explored the contributions of the Jewish diaspora to the architectural landscapes of their host countries. Having now analyzed this, and taking a step back to consider the subject from a broader perspective, we can discern two distinct periods in the history of Jewish input in architecture: one preceding the advent of Jewish emancipation in the late eighteenth and early nineteenth century.

During the first period, Jewish contributions to the architecture of host nations were primarily quantitative. When searching for commonalities in what is considered Jewish within the buildings of the Jewish diaspora during this period—Jewish heritage, such as housing or places of worship—one could identify in this architecture only one shared element: a consistent adherence to the architectural traditions and aesthetic ideals of the host nations.

In the second period, as we shall see, Jewish contributions to the architecture of host nations are characterized not only by an increased quantity of structures, related to Jews, but by the architecture's qualitative characteristics also, such as new types of buildings, use of new materials and methods of construction, leading to new forms, and a new approach to urban development, to name a few. All this happened when Jews started to get equal rights. At last they were free to participating in all social activities.[1] In countries of Christian civ-ilization, Jews who previously resided in crowded walled areas of towns, known as ghettos, and

[1] The United States was the first country (1789) to emancipate its Jews, followed by France (1791), Netherlands (1796) and other nations. Gradually, by the end of the 19th century-early 20th century, Jews had been granted full civil rights virtually worldwide: Belgium, 1830; Canada, 1832; Norway, 1851; Great Britain, 1860–1890; Italy, 1848–1870; Sweden, 1865; Aus-tro–Hungary, 1867–1918; Bulgaria, 1878; Serbia, 1878; Germany, 1871; Switzerland, 1874; the Ottoman Empire, 1908; Portugal 1910; Spain, 1910, and Russia, 1917.

were typically restricted from pursuing most professions includ-ing architecture, suddenly gained access to all avenues of occupations. In the context of the impending 19th-century Industrial Revolution, their skills in previously allowed professions to the Jews, such as trade, money exchange, pawnshops, banking, etc., became valuable assets, rendering them more competitive. The small Jewish pawnbro-kers and moneylenders, who, until then, had been confined to ghettos, stepped into the international capital market and proved themselves more experienced and inventive than their competitors, the heirs of the wealthy feudal elite. These Jews, as they shifted their efforts to commerce and industry, began to invest their vast and ever–increasing wealth in industry, transportation, trade, and traditional Jewish philanthropy.

Emancipation of the Jews not only opened new areas for their activities, it it had also seriously changed the vector of Western society's development. In this chapter, we will discuss how emancipat-ed Jews affected it and how its results led to the development of today's global society and global architecture with its new paradigm.

INDUSTRIAL REVOLUTION AND THE JEWS. Many historians and architects perceive nineteenth-century Western architecture just as a series of revivals of Greek, Gothic, and Renaissance art designs, fused with then available then engi-neering methods and materials. But in fact, it was the century of great inno-vations in architecture, such as those mentioned above: new building typol-ogy, new architectural forms, and new urban ideas. The changes that took place in Europe and America during the nineteenth century namely the Industrial Revolu-tion led to an unprecedented explosion in real estate development and urban planning. This, in turn, created, a new class of patrons, which, as we will dis-cuss below, were overwhelmingly Jews. They became the majority of architect's customers of that time, which in itself reflected society's need for a new type of a client, a capitalist. From the middle of the nineteenth century onwards, these clients contributed in every possible way to the formation of new architecture.

The emancipation of the Jews at the end of the eighteenth century coincided with the start of the Industrial Revolution. One might even suggest that emancipation triggered the Industrial Revolution.

Some people believe that the Jews did not participate in initiating this scientific-technological revolution, that they appeared from ghettos too late. However, very few would doubt that Jews furthered this revolution at its every step. Yuri Slezkine stated that "They did adjust better than most—and reshaped the modern world as a consequence—but they were not present at the creation [of it] and missed out on some of the early role assignments."[2] This assessment is based on the assumption that the Industrial Revolution started with the invention of the spinning jenny in 1764, the improvements to the steam engine in the 1770s, and the successful operation of the water-powered cotton spinning mill in 1771. However, these technological advances did not revolutionize the rate of societal development. If we examine the dynamics of the Industrial Revolution, we can see that it was only with the emergence of emancipated Jews in Western civilization, first as entrepreneurs and financiers and later as scholars, scientists, and engineers, that the rate of industrial and societal development shifted from its snail's pace of EVOLUTION in the eiteenth and early nineteenth centuries to the speed of genuine REVOLUTION by the mid-19th century. For instance, the steam engine was invented by Thomas Newcomen in 1712, the first locomotive—one hundred years later in 1812, by Matthew Murray, and finally, in 1825 George Stephenson developed a full-fledged locomotive. However, this invention began to be widely used and greatly affected the speed of the Industrial Revolution only after Jewish entrepreneurs such as the Péreire brothers and Rothschilds in Europe, and the Polyakov brothers in Russia, with their crucial financial backing started and facilitated the construction of railway networks across the continent in 1840s and 1850s.

While Jews unknowingly spurred this vast scientific–technical revolution when they emerged from the ghettos at the end of the 18th century, Western civilization was likewise prompted to come to a new philosophical understanding of reality and a new form of society— capitalism.[3] Jews were the

2 See: Slezkine, Yuri. *The Jewish Century.* Princeton University Press. 2006. P. 6.

3 See: Sombart, Werner. *The Jews and Modern Capitalism.* Batoche Books, Kitchener, Canada. 2001. Originally: *Die Juden und das Wirtschaftsleben.* Leipzig: Duncker und Humblot, 1911. Also: Muller, J. *Capitalism and the Jews.* Princeton University Press, 2011.

main force in establishing capitalism in Europe and America. Judaism and its ethics were the genesis of capitalism. As Werner Sombart noticed, "Modern capitalism is nothing more or less than an expression of the Jewish spirit."[4]

The Industrial Revolution marked a significant period of rapid advancements in science, technology, and industry. These advancements had a profound impact on societies and economies worldwide.[5] Emerged Jewish scholars played a significant role in the intellectual and scientific advancements of the Industrial Revolution, especially later in the 19th century. Among them were such scientists and engineers as mathematicians David Hilbert and Hermann Minkowski, physicists Henrietta Hertz and Paul Ehrlich, economist Oswald Veblen, and inventors Emile Berliner and Leo Baekeland, to name a few.

Throughout the 19th century, innovations spread rapidly across countries and continents, resulting in significant improvements in manufacturing processes, transportation, communication, and various other sectors. Emancipated Jewish diaspora played a key role in fueling this development, evident in the main features of the Industrial Revolution. These features included the development of a robust banking system with increased capital investment, the establishment of large-scale factories with improved access to resources due to advancements in transportation, rapid urbanization, globalization, and the dissemination of knowledge through scientific societies and publications.

There are numerous examples of Jewish industrialists who made significant contributions to several industries in the 19th century. Their entrepreneurial spirit, technological innovations, and global networks played a crucial role in shaping the industry's growth and development, leaving an enduring legacy of the Industrial Revolution. In the textile industry, there were such Jewish industrialists as Ludwig Gumpel, Solomon Oppenheim, Max Schapira, Julius Poznański, and Samuel Lazard. In iron and steel production, the crucial roles were Karl Wittgenstein, Max Hirsch, Samuel Blumenstein, Aron Hirsch Kohn, and Julius Popper. In the communication industry, there were Hermann Hirsch and Emil Berliner. Industrialists Samuel Insull, Julius

---

4 See: Sombart, p. 35.

5 At the same time, they led to economic hardships and social inequality, which triggered multiple revolutions across Europe, most notably French Revolution.

Rosenthal, Leopold Ullman, Edward Lauterbach, and Emil Rathenau developed the electrical industry. Ludwig Mond, Ernest Solvay, and Julius Fuerst are known as pioneers in the chemical industry. Such outstanding figures as Mayer Rothschild, David Sassoon, Leopold Goldschmidt, Abraham Strauss, Louis Bamberger, Julius Rosenwald, Levi Strauss, Isidor Hirsch, and Oscar Straus were behind the main innovations in the trade and banking industry. In urbanizations of Europe and America, we can find the names of Michael Reese, Leopold von Hirsch, Levi Strauss, and Oscar Straus.

In time, the changes set in motion by the Industrial Revolution would be reflected not only in science, technology, and finances, but also in literature, art, city planning, and architecture. Whereas, until the 19th century, the Jews had been virtually barred from landownership, they now moved with tremendous energy to acquire real estate. However, at the beginning of the Industrial Revolution, due to the absence of Jewish architects (a profession then devoid of Jews) Jewish presence in the real estate development was primarily observed in the role of architects' clients.

THE ROLE OF THE JEWISH CLIENT is difficult to overstate. This fact was studied in great detail in enormous as well as meticulous research by the Swedish art historian Fredric Bedoire.[6] In his remarkable work, Bedoire has analyzed with the utmost scholarly care the interaction of changes in Jewish status and the progress of the Industrial Revolution. In particular, he traced how the development of industry and a new social structure led to the disproportionate increase in Jewish participation in all spheres, especially, in real estate development. Bedoire's study showed how the transformations that took place in Europe and America during that century created a new class of patrons, mostly Jews, and allowed for an unprecedented explosion in new building types and urban planning.

For example, Bedoire refers to the above-mentioned brothers Emile and Isaac Pereire, who were railroad builders. They were also the founders of the first modern bank and the first large real estate construction company, builders of the first hotels, and the most important residential projects in Paris in the mid–19th century. Over 14 years

---

6 See: Bedoire, Fredric. *The Jewish Contribution to Modern Architecture, 1830-1930.* Jersey City: Ktav Publishing, 2004

(1852–1866), they built thousands of buildings in Paris, developing a total of about 100 kilometers of real estate along streets (Illus. 5.1.1 and 5.1.2.).[7] Theirs was one of a great many Jewish families engaged in similar undertakings throughout Europe, along with Rothschilds, Lamms, Sachses, Wittgensteins, Mendelssohns, and others.

"If the first half of the nineteenth century was dominated by the aristocrats," noticed Bedoire, "in the second it was the bourgeoisie who set the tone of things."[8] "True, there was an important Christian bourgeoisie, such as the Borsigs in Berlin and the Krupps in Essen," he argued, and concluded: "but the Jews, headed by the House of Rothschild, set the tone in many of the continental cities."[9] By then they constituted the main portion of the European bourgeoisie.

According to Bedoire's findings, Jews played a central role in the emergence of contemporary architecture in Europe by the end of the 19th Century. Bedoire discovered that in the explosion of new building types, such as railway stations, department stores, banks, office buildings, exhibition halls, movie theaters, etc., the driving force was mostly Jews. His study shows that in the 19th century all the clients of this new architecture—industrialists, town builders, and financiers—almost to a person, with rare exceptions and in all the nations of Western civilization, were Jews.

Bedoire highlighted the significant role of these Jewish patrons in shaping European and American architecture in the 19th and early 20th centuries. In Bedoire's research, we can find detailed analyses of the efforts of over two hundred outstanding Jewish clients who significantly influenced the architectural landscape in the 19th century. Along with the Pereire brothers who established a modern residential area in the heart of Paris, which came to epitomize contemporary urban living, there are the Jewish owners of the renowned department stores, Grands Magasins du Printemps (Illus. 5.1.3, 1881-1885) and Galeries Lafayette (Illus. 5.1.4, 1906-1912), Jules Jaluzot, and Alphonse Kahn and Theodor Bader, respectively. They led the way in introducing impressive iron and glass atria that quickly became emblematic of modern retail spaces, the department stores. James de Rothschild built an extravagant residence, located

---

7 Ibid, p.166
8 Ibid, p. 13
9 Ibid, p 14

5.1.1. Pereire Brothers. City development. Paris, France. 1900. Photo credit: public domain

5.1. 2. Pereire brothers. Palace Europe. Paris, France. Photo credit: Wiki, Slovenska

5.1.3. Paul Sédille. Grands Magasins du Printemps. Paris, France. Circa 1889.
Photo credit: Lleon and Levy

5.1.4. Galeries Lafayette. Paris, France. Photo credit: public domain

near Paris in Ferrieres-en-Brie, which stood out among other country homes due to its unconventional design, innovative features, and assertive presence. Berlin's Jewish industrialists and bankers erected magnificent villas alongside the Tiergarten (Illus. 5.1.5), as well as the iconic domed Oranienburgerstrasse synagogue (Illus. 5.1.6) and brought the Parisian department store concept to the German capital. Jewish individuals in Vienna played a significant role in promoting and developing the Ringstrasse (Illus. 5.1.7 and 5.1.8), constructing their palazzos in the process. The Polyakov brothers in Russia developed a network of railways along with the first railway stations and terminals (Illus. 5.1.9 and 5.1.10). The Poznanski family in Poland had built factories and one of the first workers' housing complexes (Illus. 5.1.11 and 5.1.12). Jewish industrialists and developers in North America, such as Abraham Levy, Joseph Seligman, Henry Morgenthau Sr., and Julius Rosenwald, along with others, developed cities, introduced contemporary department stores, built railways, movie theaters, and museums.

Among Jewish patrons, who played an important role in nurturing an aspiring new generation of architects, Bedoire mentions industrialist Karl Wittgenstein, who financed the Secession Movement; Ludwig Josef Johann Wittgenstein, who gifted a portion of his inheritance to Adolf Loos; Fritz Warndorfer, the most important patron of Charles Rennie Mackintosh; Tugendhat family, which financed young Mies van der Rohe, and an art collector Michel Stein, the client of the wannabe architect Le Corbusier, to cite a few.

Bedoire argues that the Western world would look very different without the contributions of Jewish clients, who were often at the forefront of commissioning innovative and complex architectural works. His research shows that Jewish clients often took a leading role in their projects, providing clear instructions to their architects while also giving them the freedom to express their creativity. For example, Jewish banker and merchant Louis Fould gave his architect Henri Labrouste a free hand in designing his house, while at the same time specifying the overall essence of what he wanted. On the other hand, Jewish patrons such as James Rothschild and Carl Robert Lamm kept their architectural projects under such close control that there was little room for the architect to exercise traditional autonomy.

5.1.5. Max Liebermann villa. Tiergarten, Berlin, Germany. Photo credit: taz.de

5.1.6. Oranienburgerstrasse synagogue. Berlin, Germany.
Photo credit: HEN-Magonza flickr.com

5.1.7. Theophil Hansen. Todesco Palace. Vienna, Austria. Photo credit: austriasites.com

5.1.8. Theophil Hansen. Epstein Palace. Vienna, Austria. Photo credit: gpsmycity.com

5.1.9. Russian railway station. 1900s. Photo credit: public domain

5.1.10. Fyodor Shekhtel. Yaroslavsky railway terminal. Moscow, Russia. 1904.
Photo credit: Legion Media rbth.com

5.1.11. Poznanski cotton mills. Lodz, Poland. 1920. Photo credit: Bronisław Wilkoszewski

5.1.12. Poznanski workers housing complex. Lodz, Poland.
Photo credit: kladkowiec.vblogspot.com

Demands of the Jewish nouveau riche differed fundamentally from those of their predecessors and generated new, never-before-seen types of buildings. As one of the subjects of architecture, typology always developed alongside new customs, traditions, ways of life, new materials and methods, etc., starting from primitive caves to primitive huts to elaborate temples. New typology is one of the precursors of a new era in architecture. Toward the end of the 18th century, when the Jews were beginning their exodus from the ghettos, building types were quite limited. Medieval castles, burgher townhouses with shops on the ground floor, small workshops, structures for religious purposes, hospitals, and homes for the poor and aged—none of these fulfilled the needs of the new society that was taking shape. In the 19th century, new types of buildings were needed for the new capitalist society: railway stations, terminals, factories, banks, residential buildings, department stores, hi-rises, subway stations, airports, office buildings, exhibition halls, workers dwellings, shopping centers, and museums. The Jewish contribution to the typology of contemporary architecture also includes planned factory towns, movie theaters, department stores, and shopping malls.

Emancipated Jews were among the first to veer sharply away from traditional thinking and behavior in all aspects of culture. In architecture, this manifested itself in the development of non–traditional types and forms of buildings. Practically, starting in the late nineteenth century almost all the groundbreaking modern architectural projects were commissioned by Jews. These new things under the sun reflected the wider, more cosmopolitan outlook of the new clientele.

For example, Otto Wagner's Majolica House (Illus. 5.1.15, 1898–1899), which Viennese society at first despised and now reveres, was commissioned by Wilhelm Frankel, a Jew. Also in Vienna are Adolf Loos' Goldman & Salatsch Building (Illus. 5.1.13 and 5.1.14, 1910) and the Steiner House (Illus. 5.1.16, 5.1.17 and 5.1.18, 1910) built for the Steiner family (Lilly and Hugo Steiner), who were Jewish. The Théâtre des Champs-Élysées in Paris (Illus. 5.1.19., 1913)—one of the first reinforced concrete buildings, designed by Auguste Perret and Gustave Perret—was commissioned by Gabriel Astuce, who was Jewish.

5.1.13. Adolf Loos. Goldman & Salatsch building. Vienna, Austria.
Photo credit: archdaily.com

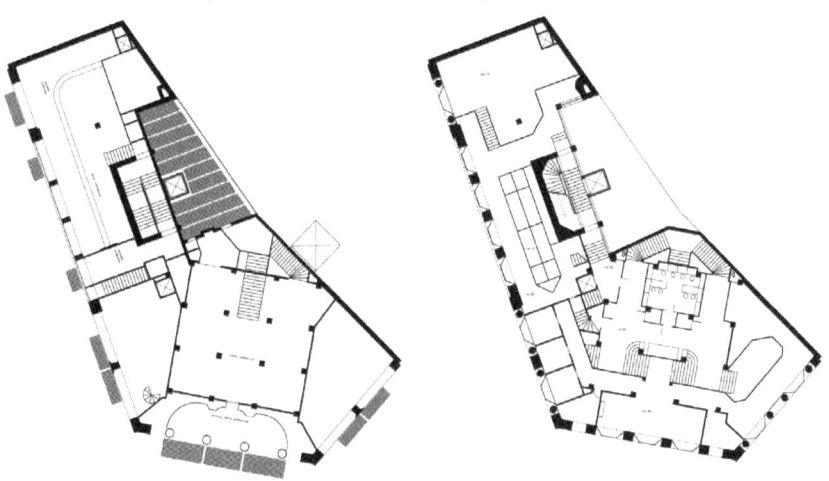

5.1.14. Adolf Loos. Goldman & Salatsch building. Vienna, Austria. Floor plans.
Photo credit: urbipedia.org

5.1.15. Otto Wagner. Majolica House. Vienna, Austria. Photo credit: wga.hu

5.1.16. Adolf Loos. Steiner House. Vienna, Austria. Photo credit: darquitectura.tumblr.com

5.1.17. Adolf Loos. Steiner House. Vienna, Austria. Photo credit: pinterest.co.kr.

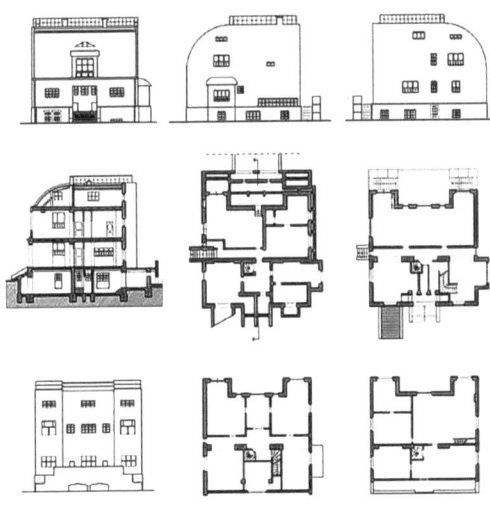

5.1.18. Adolf Loos. Steiner House. Vienna, Austria. Drawings. Photo credit: pinterest.co.kr

Landmark groundbreaking buildings of the first half of the 20th century commissioned by Jews include such iconic projects as the Villa Savoye (Illus. 5.1.20, 1928), built for the owner of an insurance company, Pierre Savoy, and his wife, Emilie, by the architect Le Corbusier. No less significant icon of contemporary architecture, the residential Glass House, or Maison de Verre (Illus. 5.1.21 and 5.1.22, 1928–1932), was designed by Perré Chareau, Bernard Bijvoet, and Louis Dalbet for the Dalsace family (Annie and Jean Dalsace).

Young Mies Van der Rohe, later—one of the leading 20th-century architects, designed landmark villas for the Riehl, Wolf, and Perl families (Illus. 5.1.23, 1907, 5.1.24, 1922 and 5.1.28, 1911), and an iconic modernist villa for Grete and Fritz Tugendhat (Illus. 5.1.25 and 5.1.26, 1930). Later on, at the height of his career, he designed the milestone Seagram Building in New York (Illus. 5.1.27, 1958)—for the Samuel Bronfman family.

Other landmark designs of modern architecture commissioned by Jewish clients include the Villa Meyer (Illus. 5.1.29, 1925–1926, unbuilt), and the Villa Stein (Illus. 5.1.30, 1923 and 5.1.31, 1927), both by young Le Corbusier; the Galerie Bernheim and Galerie Paul Rosenberg in Paris (1925) and the Villa Guggenbuhl (Illus. 5.1.32 and 5.1.33, 1927), designed by architect Andre Lurcat. In the United States, there is Frank Lloyd Wright's Fallingwater (Illus. 5.1.34 and 5.1.35, 1936–1939), designed for the Kaufmann family, and his Solomon Guggenheim Museum (Illus. 5.1.36, 5.1.37 and 5.1.38, 1959) in New York, designed for the Guggenheim family.

By the end of the 20th century, additional landmark modern buildings for Jewish clients arrived. Among them: John Hancock Center (Illus. 5.1.39 and 5.1.40 1969) in Chicago, by SOM—for Jerry Wolman, Jerry Wolman Associates; Franklin Center (Illus. 5.1.41, 1989) in Chicago, by SOM—for Robert Tishman and Jerry Speyer, Tishman Speyer Properties; the Guggenheim Museum (Illus. 5.1.42 and 5.1.43, 1997) in Bilbao, Spain, designed by Frank Gehry and commissioned by the Guggenheims.

What is important to emphasize, all these structures are leading, groundbreaking exemplars of global contemporary architecture. In both Europe and the United States, there were now many ultra-rich individuals of all backgrounds. Yet, as with the first collectors

5.1.19. Auguste Perret and Gustave Perret. The Théâtre des Champs-Élysées. Paris, France. Photo credit: europexlo.com

5.1.20. Le Corbusier. Villa Savoye. Poissy, France. Photo credit: lesbonnesvisites.com

5.1.21. Pierre Chareau and Bernard Bijvoet, Maison de Verre. Paris, France.
Photo credit: angioinfo.com

5.1.22. Pierre Chareau and Bernard Bijvoet. Maison de Verre. Paris, France.
Photo credit: yellowtrace.com

5.1.23. Mies Van der Roe. The Alois and Sophie Riehl House. Potsdam, Germany. 1907.
Photo credit: George Smart

5.1.24. Mies Van der Roe. The Erich Wolf House. Guben, Germany. 1922.
Photo credit: George Smart

5.1.25. Mies Van der Roe. Tugendhat house. Brno, Czech Republic. 1930. Street view.
Photo credit: behance.net

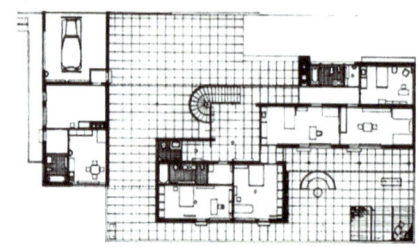

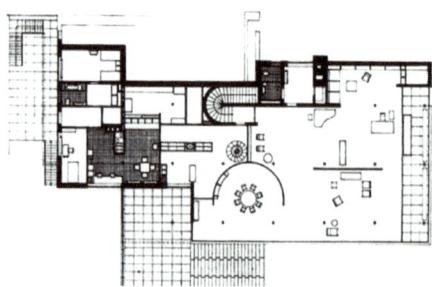

5.1.26. Mies Van der Roe. Tugendhat house. Brno, Czech Republic. 1930. Floor plans.
Photo credit: homedecor208.netiify

5.1.27. Mies Van der Roe. Seagram building. New York. 1958.
Photo credit: Ezra Stoller archeyes.com

5.1.28. Mies Van der Roe. Villa Perl. Berlin. 1911. Street view. Photo credit: impressum

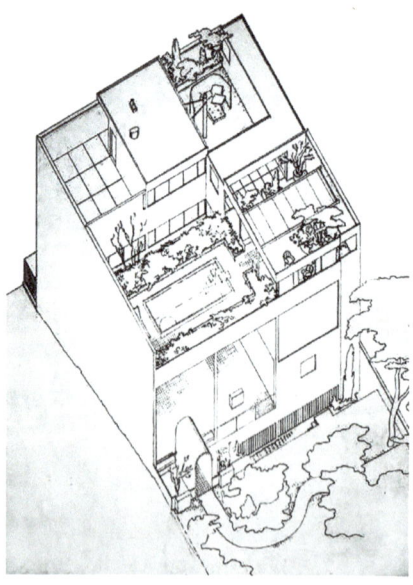

5.1.29. Le Corbusier. Villa Meyer. 1925. Unbuilt. Photo credit: foundation lecorbusier.fr

5.1.30. Le Corbusier. Villa Stein. Garches, France. 1928. Street view.
Photo credit Tim Benton.visuallexicon.worldpress.com.

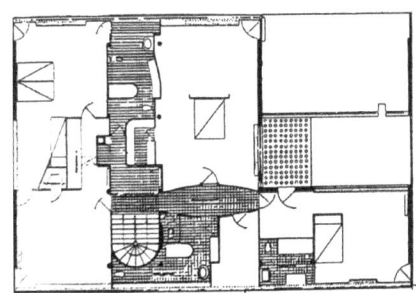 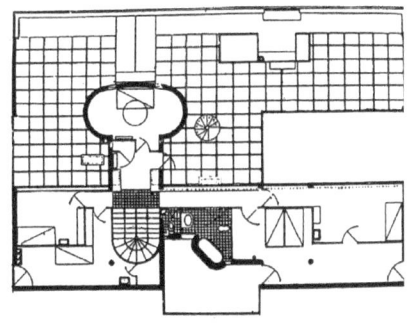

5.1.31. Le Corbusier. Villa Stein. Garches, France. 1928. Floor plans.
Photo cfredit: W.Boesiger and H. Girsberger.visuallexicon.worldpress.com

5.1.32. Andre Lurcat. Villa Guggenbuhl. Paris. France. 1926-1927.
Street view. Photo credit: Bonney, Therese library.si.edu

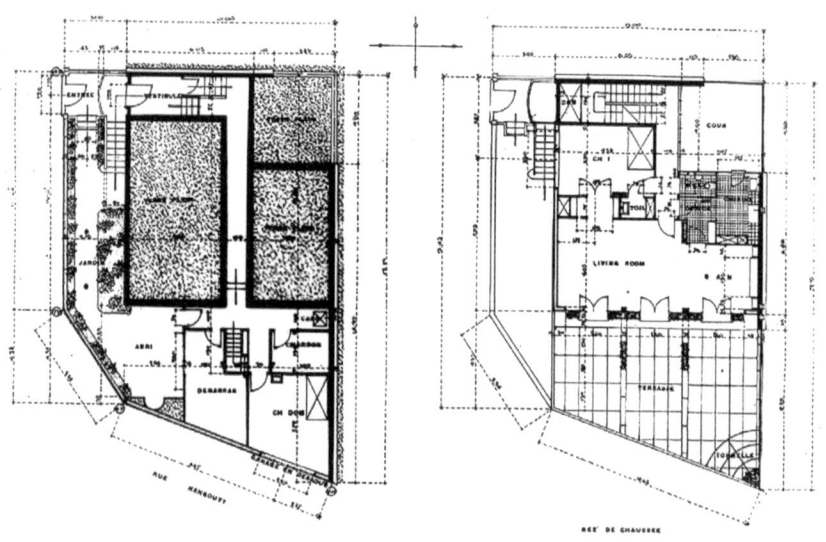

5.1.33. Andre Lurcat. Villa Guggenbuhl. Paris. France. 1926-1927.
Floor Plans. Photo credit urbipedia.org

5.1.34. Frank Lloyd Wright. Fallingwater. Bear Run, Pennsylvania. USA. 1935. Photo credit: Jene J. Puskar.wesa.fm

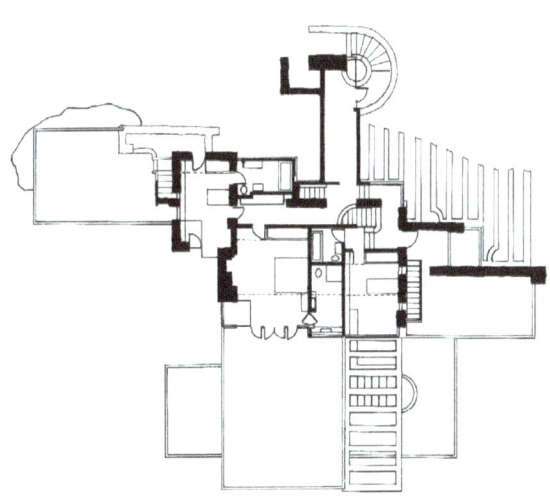

5.1.35. Frank Lloyd Wright. Fallingwater. Bear Run, Pennsylvania. USA. 1935. Floor plan. Photo credit: housedesignideas.us

5.1.36. Frank Lloyd Wright. Guggenheim Museum. New York. USA. 1959.
Photo by author

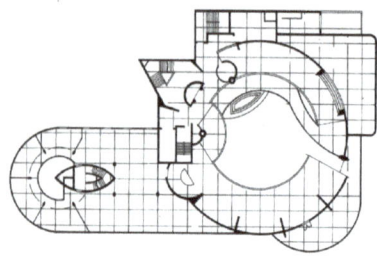

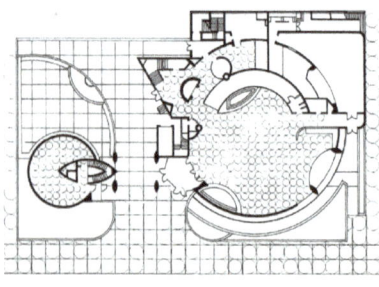

5.1.37. Frank Lloyd Wright. Guggenheim Museum. New York. USA. 1959. Floor plans. Photo credit: McCarter, R. visuallexicon. worldpress.com

5.1.38. Frank Lloyd Wright. Guggenheim Museum. New York. USA. 1959. Interior. Photo by author.

5.1.39. Bruce Graham. John Hancock Building, Chicago. USA. 1965. Photo credit: Y.C.Liu

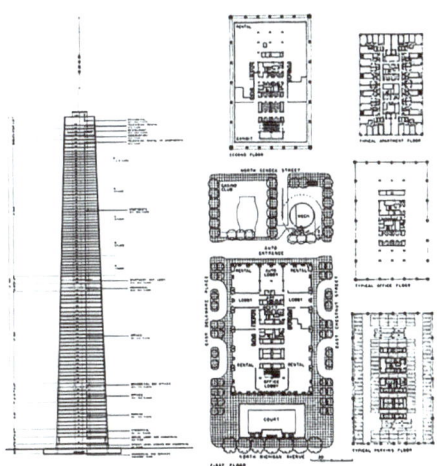

5.1.40. Bruce Graham. John Hancock Building, Chicago. USA. 1965. Floor plans. Section. Photo credit: 100 Years of Architecture in Chicago, flickriver.com

of groundbreaking art, which we will discuss in a moment, the great commissions for mold-breaking contemporary architecture mainly came from persons of Jewish background.

It's not about how individual Jews, customers, and architects participated in the formation of modern architecture of the West (although it was of great importance), as precursors of a new, global architecture, but about how closely the history of the Jewish people over the past two centuries is connected with the emergence and development of the base and conditions for the birth and flourishing of the architecture of the 20th–21st centuries.

ARTISTIC MOVEMENTS IN LATE 19TH—EARLY 20TH–CENTURY were other precursors of a new era in architecture. The 19th century was a period of significant artistic innovations and changes in both Europe and America. Several important art movements emerged during this time, each with its distinctive characteristics and contributions: Neoclassicism, Romanticism, Realism, Impressionism, Post-Impressionism, Symbolism, Arts and Crafts, and Art Nouveau, among others. These movements represented a diverse range of styles and philosophies in 19th-century European and American art. They reflected the cultural, social, and political changes of the time and continue to influence art to this day. Two of them, Arts and Crafts (1880–1910) and Art Nouveau (1890–1910) although being pure art movements served as precursors of the coming new architectural language.

The Arts and Crafts movement can be characterized as a reaction against the effects of the Industrial Revolution

5.1.41. SOM. Franklin Center. Chicago, USA. 1989. Photo credit: JoeRockEHF

5.1.42. Frank Gehry. Guggenheim Museum. Bilbao, Spain. 1997. Photo by author.

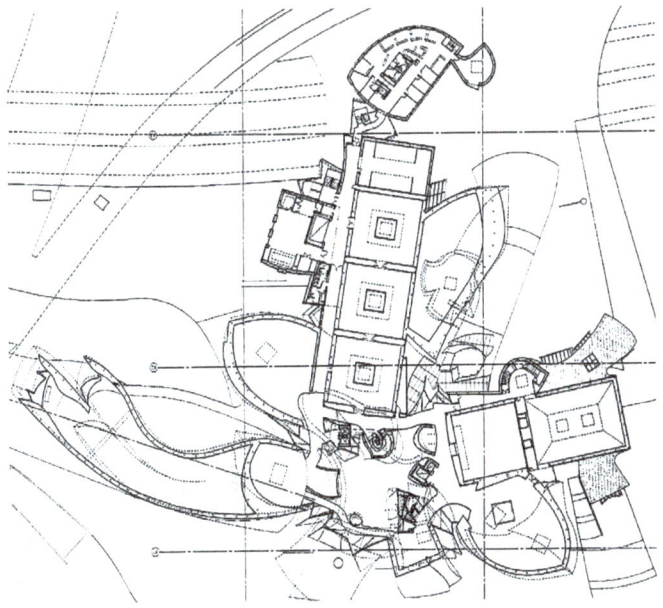

5.1.43. Frank Gehry. Guggenheim Museum. Bilbao. Spain. 1997. Floor plan.
Photo credit: inexhibit.com

and the mass production of goods. It emphasized a return to handcrafted, high-quality, and aesthetically pleasing objects, and advocated for skilled craftsmanship, quality materials, and attention to detail. It rejected the soulless and often shoddy products of industrial mass production. Several notable artists, designers, and architects were associated with the Arts and Crafts movement. Among them were: one of the founders of the 'Arts and Crafts' movement, William Morris; an influential art critic and writer John Ruskin; Scottish architect and designer Charles Rennie Mackintosh; an American furniture designer and maker Gustav Stickley; an English designer, and entrepreneur C.R. Ashbee; an English architect and designer Arthur Heygate Mackmurdo; and a Scottish artist and designer Margaret Macdonald Mackintosh (Illus. 5.2.2). Their impact on architecture and interior design was in its principles of simplicity, functional design, and handmade materials being applied to buildings and home furnishings (Illus. 5.2.1.).

Another movement among precursors of the coming new architectural language, is known as Art Nouveau in France and Belgium, Jugendstil in Germany, Secession in Austria, Modernisme in Spain, and Modern in Russia. It was a significant art and design drive that emerged in the late 19th century and lasted into the early 20th century. Art Nouveau has its roots in Belgium. In the 1880s, the creative endeavors of a collective of Belgian painters and sculptors known as Les Vingt, who were fervently advocating for a transformation in the world of art, were dubbed Art Nouveau by a local art journal. However, it wasn't until 1895 that the Art Nouveau movement truly took flight. This pivotal moment came when Siegfried Bing, a Jewish artist and art dealer, inaugurated an art salon in Paris, christened the 'Maison de l'Art Nouveau,' meaning the 'House of the New Art.' For the revamp of the salon's façade (Illus. 5.2.3 and 5.2.4.), he enlisted the talents of artist Frank Brangwyn, alongside architects Louis Bonnier and Victor Horta. The salon attracted a diverse array of budding artists from various nations, with luminaries such as Charles Tiffany from the United States and Henry van de Velde from Belgium among its prominent participants.

Art Nouveau was characterized by its ornate, decorative style, including sinuous lines, intricate patterns, and a strong emphasis on nature and organic forms. Art Nouveau represented a departure from the academic and historicist art styles of the 19th century and it laid the foundation for subsequent art movements, such as Art Deco, and some elements of modern design. It celebrated the idea of total art, where design was integrated into all aspects of daily life, from architecture and furniture to posters and jewelry.

Jews played a significant role in these movements. No wonder. As Joseph Jacobs mentions, during the centuries Jews were constantly involved in all sorts of similar activities. "For nearly two thousand years they have taken their share in all the movements that have made the modern European man. At times they have helped to spread culture from one nation to another; at others, they have helped to light it anew in a fresh land. On some occasions, they have even been leaders in these movements, but mostly they have been content to take their share in the cultural development of their fellow men, contributing to it by the qualities which their unique position among the nations had developed in them."[10] According to Frederick Bedoire, already at the beginning of its fame, the Art Nouveau movement, "and its symbolic vocabulary were being interpreted as Jewish. The same was true of the Viennese 'Secession,' which, when presented in Paris at the 1900 World Exhibition attracted a great deal of attention—but as a goût juif, Jewish taste."[11] Art Nouveau was rejected by all the 'enlightened' part of contemporary society, except Jews. Bedoire testified that "almost everywhere on the Continent, emancipated Jews were associated with the origins of the Art Nouveau, or Jugendstil, aesthetic."[12] The Jews were the people who were actively promoting these new trends in art. Bedoire describes numerous places in Europe where Jews and Jewish artists made this happen: Paris, Berlin, Vienna, Lemberg (Lvov), Czernowitz (Cernauti), Stockholm, and Riga, among others.

There were many Jewish artists and architects who were associated with the new trend, and made notable contributions to it. Among them were such luminaries as French architect Hector Guimard; a Jewish artist and illustrator

---

10   Jacobs, Joseph. *Jewish contribution to civilization: an estimate.* The Jewish Publication Society of America. Philadelphia. 1919. P. 11.

11   Bedoire, p. 494
12   Ibid, p. 495

5.2.1. Gustav Stickley furniture. Photo credit: Pilar Simon artsandcraftshomes.com

5.2.2. Margaret Macdonald Mackintosh. The May Queen (detail). 1900.
Photo credit: cabq.gov

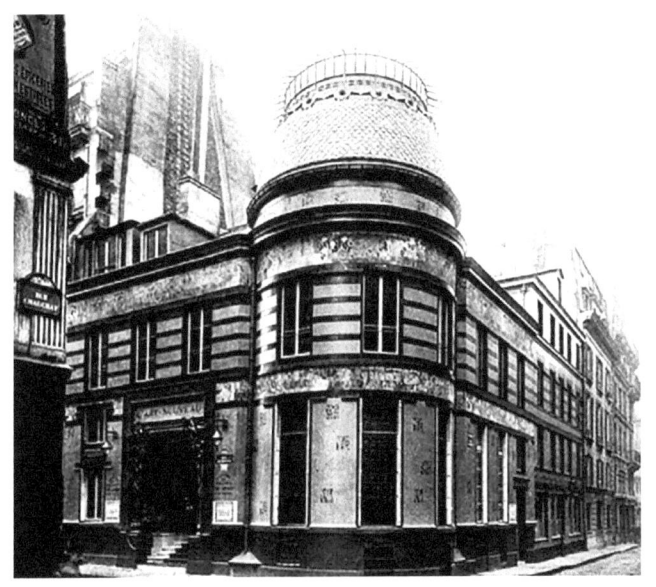

5.2.3. Siegfried Bing. Maison de l'Art Nouveau. Paris 1895. Photo credit: ccfjt.com

5.2.4. Siegfried Bing. Maison de l'Art Nouveau. Paris. 1895.
Photo credit: Lorena Pimentel Arana at mueble-enlahistoria.blogspot.com

Ephraim Moses Lilien; an Austrian-Jewish painter Max Kurzweil; a German-Jewish artist Hermann Struck; and a graphic and interior designer Koloman Moser. Many notable non-Jewish artists and designers like a Czech artist known for his iconic posters, Alphonse Mucha (Illus. 5.2.5); the Austrian symbolist painter Gustav Klimt, the French painter Henri de Toulouse-Lautrec, a French glass artist and furniture designer Émile Gallé, an American artist and design-er Louis Comfort Tiffany, a Spanish architect Antoni Gaudí, a French glass designer and jeweler René Lalique, an English illustrator and author Aubrey Beardsley, a Scottish architect Charles Rennie Mackintosh, and others were associated with the Art Nouveau movement also.

Wealthy industrialists and entrepreneurs from Europe and the United States along with many not-so-wealthy individual art collectors and enthusiasts, acquired Art Nouveau works for their personal collections. Among them were such art collectors as the prominent German industrialist Krupp family in Germany, the tire company Michelin family in France, the prominent American Vanderbilt family in the United States, as well as the Grand Ducal Family of Luxembourg and Grand Duke Mikhail Aleksandrovich of Russia.

However, most of these art collectors started to buy Art Nouveau works when it became fashionable and valuable.

On the other hand, Jewish patrons greatly supported, and even more—they nurtured participating artists of Arts and Crafts and Art Nouveau movements at the start when society at large rejected it. A Jewish banker from Vienna, entrepreneur, patron of the arts, and founding member of the Wiener Werkstätte, Fritz Warndorfer was the most important patron of Rennie Mackintosh. A German-born Jewish steel tycoon in Austria industrialist Karl Wittgenstein and an Austrian industrialist August Lederer supported artists of the Secession movement. Jewish clients of Art Nouveau artists include also the Jewish-American novelist, poet, playwright, and art connoisseur Gertrude Stein, and members of such wealthy Jewish families as the prominent art collectors and gallery owners in France, Bernheim-Jeun, art collectors and patrons of the Art Nouveau movement Salomon family, and Rothschilds, who were known to acquire and commission Art Nouveau works.

There were also numerous not-so-wealthy Jewish individuals with a passion for Art Nouveau. Many of these art

5.2.5. Alphonse Mucha. Flower. 1897. Photo credit: public domain

collectors were murdered by the Nazis, while their collections were looted.[13]

The unique style of Art Nouveau found expression in various artistic disciplines and had a significant impact on the visual arts and architecture of the late 19th and early 20th centuries. The key aspects of the Art Nouveau movement, like asymmetric design and use of new materials and techniques, including glass, wrought iron, ceramics, and stained glass, had a strong influence on design, especially on form creation in architecture.

The dawn of the 20th century was a period of many artistic innovations and experimentation, with several influential art movements that emerged in Europe and the United States: Fauvism, Cubism, Expressionism, Surrealism, Dada, Suprematism, Constructivism, Bauhaus, De Stijl, and Abstract Expressionism. The art movements that had the most profound impact on contemporary architecture language were Suprematism, Constructivism, Bauhaus, and Art Deco.

Suprematism is an abstract art movement that emerged in Russia around 1915, and it is characterized by non-objective, geometric compositions, often featuring basic shapes such as squares, circles, and rectangles, and a limited palette of colors, typically dominated by white, black, and primary colors. Suprematism had a notable influence on architecture during the early 20th century, particularly through its emphasis on abstract, geometric forms and the idea of reducing art and design to their purest, most essential elements. While not as dominant in architectural practice as in the visual arts, Suprematist principles did inspire architects and design movements, leading to the creation of buildings and structures that reflected the movement's aesthetic concepts.

Some Jewish artists played significant roles in the development of Suprematism. Among them were: a Jewish artist, designer, and architect El Lissitzky (Illus. 5.2.6 and 5.2.7); a Jewish artist, one of Malevich's favorite students Lazar Khidekel' (5.2.8 and 5.2.9); a Jewish artist Ilya Chashnik; and a Jewish artist of Ukrainian origin Natan Altman. Jewish artists played a significant role

---

13 Among them were Carl Sachs, Alfred Flechtheim, Franz Friedrich Grünbaum, Karl Mayländer, Oscar Reichel, Heinrich Rieger, Eleonore Stiassny, Heinrich Tannhäuser and others, who acquired works by Edvard Munch, Henri de Toulouse-Lautrec, Gustav Klimt, Egon Schiele, Oskar Kokoschka, Pablo Picasso, Georges Braque, Max Liebermann, Max Beckmann, Juan Gris, and Alphonse Mucha.

in shaping the development of Suprematism and the broader avant-garde landscape, contributing to the innovative and experimental spirit of the early 20th century.

Suprematist artists' use of basic geometric shapes, such as squares, circles, and rectangles, inspired architects to explore similar geometric abstractions in their designs. Suprematism, with its emphasis on bold, monumental forms and the use of large, simple shapes, influenced the design of public buildings and monuments. These structures often featured massive, abstract geometries and a sense of grandeur. Suprematism played a significant role in the development of the Constructivist architectural movement. Architects like El Lissitzky and Lazar Khidekel' were associated with both movements and integrated Suprematist principles into their Constructivist designs.

While the direct architectural manifestations of Suprematism may not have been as widespread as other design movements like the Bauhaus or Art Deco, its emphasis on abstraction, geometry, and the search for a new, non-representational architectural language left a lasting impact on modern architecture. It contributed to the evolution of architectural thinking, particularly in the context of early 20th-century avant-garde design.

The Constructivist art movement, which emerged in Russia in the early 20th century, was characterized by its emphasis on abstraction, geometric shapes, the use of industrial materials and geometric forms, and a focus on functional, utilitarian design. Artists like Vladimir Tatlin and Aleksandr Rodchenko played significant roles in Constructivism. Several Jewish artists were associated with the Constructivist movement also, making significant contributions to its development. Among them were El Lissitzky, Natan Altman, Ilya Chashnik, along Jewish-French artist Sonia De-launay. The Jewish artists associated with Constructivism were part of a broader community of avant-garde artists in Russia during the early 20th century. They contributed to the development of modernist art, design, and architecture, leaving a lasting impact on the history of 20th-century art.

The Bauhaus, a renowned and influential school of art, design, and architecture founded in Germany in 1919, and active until 1933, had a lasting influence on architecture and design. Analogous-

5.2.6. El Lissitzky. 10 Kestnermappe Proun. 1923. Photo credit: Google_Art_Project

5.2.7. El Lissitzky. Proun 30 T. 1920s. Photo credit: wikiart.org

5.2.8. Lazar Khidekel. Suprematist Composition. 1920s. Photo credit: lazar-khidekel.

5.2.9. Lazar Khidekel. Composition. 1920s. Photo credit: mutualart.com

ly to the Arts and Crafts, the Bauhaus aimed to unify and blur the boundaries between art, craft, and technology and was a crucible for modernist ideas in architecture and design. It combined craftsmanship with modern technology. The school encouraged collaboration between artists, architects, and craftsmen to create cohesive, aesthetically pleasing designs. The Bauhaus school and its principles had a global impact. After its closure, many of its faculty and students fled Nazi persecution, and their ideas and designs spread to other parts of the world.

The Bauhaus had a diverse and international community of students and faculty. Prominent Bauhaus figures included architect Walter Gropius and artist Wassily Kandinsky. Jewish artists, along with others, were integral to the vibrant and diverse artistic environment of the Bauhaus. Among them were textile artist Anni Albers; artist and educator László Moholy-Nagy; and designer and architect Marcel Breuer. They helped shape the school's commitment to the integration of art and technology, the exploration of new materials and forms, and the development of modernist design principles that continue to influence art, design, and architecture today.

Art Deco was another influential artistic and design movement that emerged in the early 20th century, peaking in popularity during the 1920s and 1930s. It was characterized by its emphasis on luxury, modernity, geometric shapes, and a blend of various artistic styles. Art Deco found expression in a wide range of art forms, including fashion, visual arts, industrial design, film and cinema, jewelry, and interior design. Some of its major representatives include a Russian-born French artist and designer Erté (Romain de Tirtoff), fashion designers Coco Chanel, Paul Poiret, and Émile-Jacques Ruhlmann. Among the famous Jewish artists of the Art Deco movements was Polish painter, Tamara de Lempicka (Illus. 5.2.10).

Art Deco had a great influence on the development of 20th-century architectural language. An offshoot of Art Deco, the Streamline Moderne style which was characterized by curved, aerodynamic forms applied to objects like trains, cars, and household appliances was a form inspiration for many buildings of its time. One of the most famous examples of Streamline Moderne's influence on contemporary architectural language is the Union Terminal in Cincinnati, Ohio, USA (Illus. 5.2.11). It features a sweeping, curved façade. Art Deco's influence could be seen also in contemporary interiors, which were characterized by the use of rich materials like exotic woods, lacquer, and chrome, as well as geometric patterns and stylized motifs.

All these early 20th-century art movements were characterized by a spirit of innovation, a departure from traditional artistic conventions, and a desire to explore new ways of representing the world, emotions, and the human experience.

Although there were relatively few influential Jewish artists participating in these art movements, the Jews played a significant role in the development of the movements. Patrons and financiers, such as Rothschilds, Fritz Warndorfer, August Lederer, Gertrude Stein, Bernheim-Jeun, and Salomon families, Baron Raoul Kuffner, Solomon R. Guggenheim, Raymond Nasher and his wife Patsy, and Helena Rubinstein, to name a few, made art works from the movements' artists a major part of their art collections. Supporting and nurturing emerging avant-garde artists, these people were at the cradle of one of the major precursors of contemporary architecture, the artistic movements of the late nineteenth–early twentieth centuries. Thanks to the efforts of all these people, modern art became "Jewish." Charles Dellheim notices that "for the first time in the history of art a cluster of Jewish outsiders came to play pivotal roles as artists, collectors, dealers, and critics. Camille Pissarro, Max Lieber-mann, Amedeo Modigliani, Chaim Soutine, Marc Chagall, and Jacques Lip-chitz all became notable artists who took up the challenge to 'show us the face of modern Man,' as the leaders of the Vi-enna Secession put it. Pierre Loeb, who represented the surrealists in his gallery on the Left Bank, claimed that four of five avant-garde art dealers in Paris in the years between the two world wars were Jews. The number sounds high, but so was the impact of those who champi-oned successive schools of modern art. Picasso, who had nearly as many dealers as lovers, went from one Jewish dealer to another. Among the adventurous collectors who patronized the most advanced forms of modern art in the early years of the twentieth century were a small band of American Jewish expatriates: Leo and Gertrude Stein, their Baltimore friends Etta and Claribel Cone, and, later, Peggy Guggenheim. Other Jews found

5.2.10. Tamara De Lempicka. Portrait of Prince Eristoff. 1925. Photo credit: wikiart

5.2.11. Cincinnati railway terminal. 1933. Photo credit: public domain

their place in the modern movement as art critics, as did Claude-Roger Marx, Waldemar George, Louis Vauxcelles (Louis Meyer), and André Salmon."[14]

THE LANGUAGE OF MODERN ARCHITECTURE. Altogether, artistic movements of the early 20th century had a profound and lasting impact and were extremely instrumental in the development of this century's architectural language. It now included principles of simplicity, functional design (Illus. 5.3.1, Arts and Crafts); asymmetric forms, use of new materials and techniques, including wrought iron, ceramics, and stained glass (Illus. 5.3.2, Art Nouveau); abstract, geometric outlines (Illus. 5.3.3, Suprematism); use of industrial materials and geometric forms and a focus on functional, utilitarian design (Illus. 5.3.4, Constructivism); integration of art and technology, the exploration of new materials and forms (Illus. 5.3.5, Bauhaus); emphasis on modernity, geometric shapes, and a blend of various artistic styles (Illus. 5.3.6, Art Deco); and curved, aerodynamic forms (Illus. 5.3.7, Streamline Moderne).

---

14   See: Dellheim, Charles. *Belonging and Betrayal. How Jews Made the Art World Modern.* Brandeis University Press, MA. 2021.

By the end of the century, a new, revolutionary trend in architecture emerged, the architectural version of Art Nouveau. Its signal characteristic was a clear rejection of any obligation to use historical styles. As with early Gothic architecture, the basis of the new approach was harmony of function and form. That new movement in architecture suggested designing from the inside out, using new technologies (reinforced concrete, steel frames, glass surfaces), a preference for supposedly natural curved contours over straight lines and right angles, and a freer hand with space, resulting in open plans. There was also a new and profound interest in applied art (ceramics, majolica, furniture). The new trend had declared itself in Vienna with the building by Joseph Maria Olbrich for the exhibition of the Secession artists (Illus. 5.3.8 and 5.3.9), which promoted art and architecture that would celebrate modernity. As part of this exhibition the Scottish architect, Charles Rennie Mackintosh presented his avant-garde designs for the School of Art in Glasgow (Illus. 5.3.10 and 5.3.11) and for the Hillhouse mansion in Helensburgh (Illus. 5.3.12 and 5.3.13). The Austrian, Josef Hoffmann showed his design for his famed Purkersdorf Sanatorium (Illus.

5.3.1. Geometric armchair. Arts and Crafts. 1800s. Photo credit: cogpunksteamscribe. worldpress.com

5.3.2. Gate. Art Nouveau. Paris, France. Photo credit: expatwithkidsinparis.blogspot.com

5.3.3. El Lissitzky. Proun.1E. 1920. Photo credit: cristies.com

5.3.4. Vladimir Tatlin. Corner Counter-Relief, 1914. Photo credit: public domain

5.3.5. Bauhaus. Marianne Brandt. Tea infuser and strainer. 1924.
Photo credit: Colin Marshall openculture.com

5.3.6. Egyptian reeds on the
Chrysler building elevator doors.
Photo credit: 99designs.com via pinimg.

5.3.7. Streamline modern. NY
Worlds Fair 1939-1940.
Photo credit: public domain

5.3.8. Joseph Maria Olbrich. Secession Building. Vienna, Austria. 1898. Street view.
Photo credit: John Lorrd

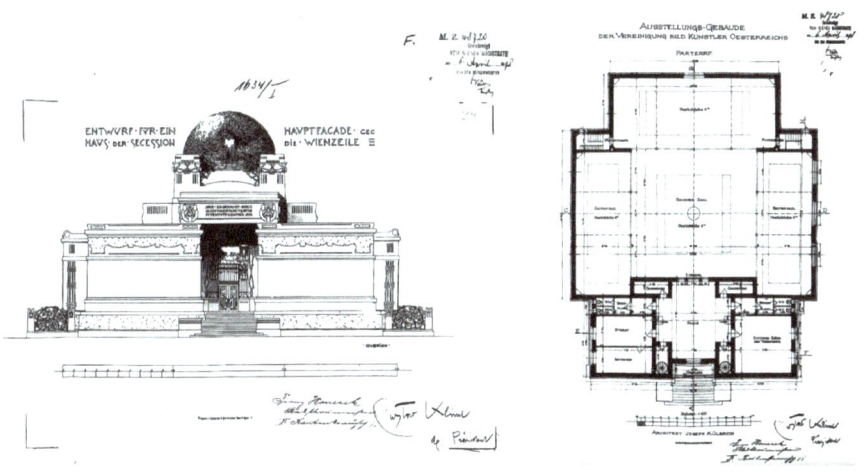

5.3.9. Joseph Maria Olbrich. Secession Building. Vienna, Austria. 1898. Elevation and plan.
Photo credit: Secession Archive

5.3.10. Charles Rennie Mackintosh. Glasgow School of Art. 1899-1909. Street view.
Photo credit: Jörg Bittner Unna

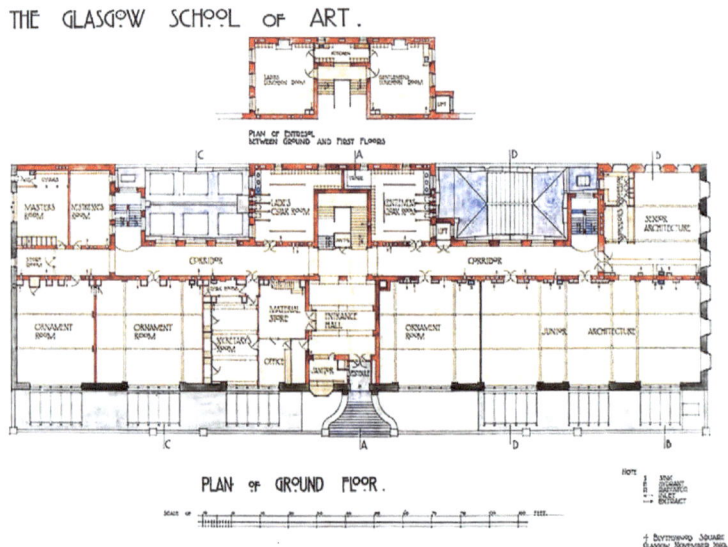

5.3.11. Charles Rennie Mackintosh. Glasgow School of Art. 1899-1909. Ground floor plan.
Photo credit: Elaine Mackenzie

5.3.12. Charles Rennie-Mackintosh. Hill House. Helensburgh, Scotland. 1902. Street view.
Photo credit: britainsfinest.co.uk

5.3.13. Charles Rennie Mackintosh. Hill House. Helensburgh, Scotland. 1902. Floor plans.
Photo credit: britainsfinest.co.uk

5.3.14. Josef Hoffmann. Sanatorium Purkersdorf. 1905. Street view.
Photo credit: es.wikiarquitectura.com

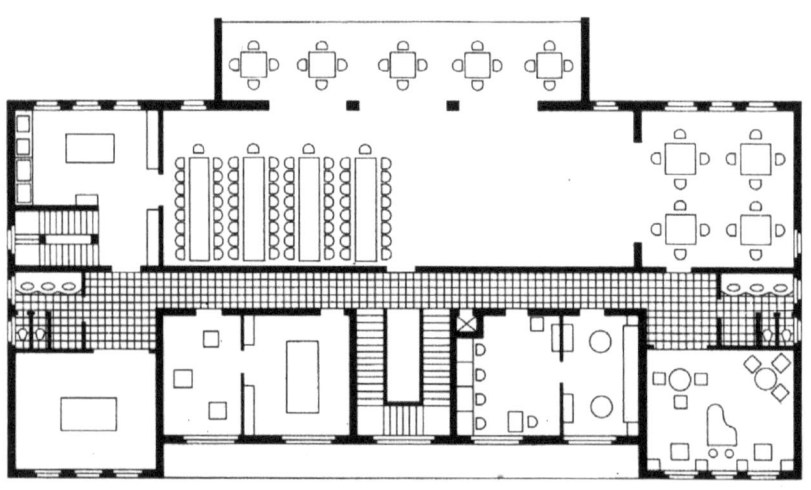

5.3.15. Josef Hoffmann. Sanatorium Purkersdorf. 1905. Floor plan.
Photo credit: en.wikiarquitectura.com

5.3.14 and 5.3.15, 1905, client Victor Zuckerkandl, a Jew). All these structures manifested the arrival of a new age of architecture. This new age developed its new language. The results of the search and experiments of artists and sculptors of artistic movements in the late 19th and early 20th centuries became the foundation of this language. It included open-spaced plans, streamlined forms, the absence of historicism and decoration, and the use of new materials like concrete, steel, and glass. This language suited well the new, unknown types of buildings and structures, exploiting new materials and construction methods to fulfill emerged customer requirements.

However, most architects of the 19th century, raised on the idea of architecture as a way of beautifying structures, still decorated their buildings with elements of different historical styles. Although they did it more frivolously. But, when they were faced with completely new types of buildings, which appeared by the middle of the century, such as hospitals, railways, railway bridges and stations, warehouses, factories, and administrative centers, they were confused. It is remarkable that in the process of evaluating projects at architectural competitions at that time building plans received very serious attention. It was happening because for their new breed of clients, who were, in fact, the partners in the process of developing projects, the functional validity of projects was very important. To compete, the common practice for architectural offices was to have an engineer do the plans, while architects resorted to the decoration of façades. Also, the architects of the 19th century were eager to delegate their work to specialists from other areas, people like the gardener Joseph Paxton (Illus. 5.3.16, The Crystal Palace, 1851), or engineers like Isambard Kingdom Brunel (Illus. 5.3.17, Paddington Station in London, 1854), or Thomas Cubit (Illus. 5.3.18, Kings Cross Station in London, 1852), or Thomas Telford (Illus. 5.3.19, St. Katharine Dock Warehouses in London, 1850s), or Gustav Eiffel (Illus. 5.3.20, Eiffel Tower, 1889), to name a few. On the other hand, the appearance of these structures helped to generate new formal architectural ideas. New social and economic changes resulted in new formal solutions, where simple, rational forms were gradually coming to be valued over traditional, classical forms.

5.3.16. Cristal Palace, London, UK. 1851. Photo credit: reddit.com

5.3.17. Paddington Station. London. UK. 1854. Interior. Photo credit: public domain

5.3.18. Kings Cross Station. London. UK. 1852. Interior. Photo credit: public domain

5.3.19. Ivory House, St. Katharine Docks. London, UK. 1858. Photo credit: novaloca.com

5.3.20. Eiffel Tower, Paris, France. 1889.
Photo credit: abcnew.go.com

JEWISH ARCHITECTS. So far, in this chapter, we exemplified the role of Jewish clients and the role of artistic movements in the development of contemporary architecture along with its language. Further development of Industrial Revolution events brought Jewish architects on to the historical scene. Their role in evolving the so-called international architecture as a precursor of contemporary architecture deserves to be illuminated.

For almost two millennia Jews had been deprived of virtually all civil rights. As a despised people fearful of expulsion, they could have no confidence in how long they might be able to stay in any one place. Such conditions hardly favored the blossoming of building occupations among the Jews. The history of Western civilization includes few names of Jewish architects before the 19th century, and that was likely to have been the case because the profession virtually required conversion to Christianity. So, one can hardly find a Jewish architect among the builders of the Middle Ages or Renaissance or at least one who had not converted. What little information exists about such individuals is fragmentary.

Over the past 150–200 years, architecture has radically changed. No longer just an adjunct to the construction business, used mainly in the decoration of buildings during the Renaissance architecture and derivatives of its era, architecture has to its original mission from prehistoric times: a field of human activity aimed at creating material habitat. As we discussed earlier, this transforma-tion owes its origin to the worldwide Industrial Revolution that began in the 18th century and continues to this day. At first, to design new types of structures, Jewish nouveau riches were commissioning contemporary non-Jewish architects for Jewish architects did not exist. Fifty years later, architects of Jewish origin appeared. After another half a century, they began to play a prominent role on the world stage.

Names of Jewish architects begin to turn up with some frequency from about the start of the 19th century. With the granting of civil rights to Jews, a process that spread through the nations of Europe and the Americas from 1789, came the emergence of Jewish architects. Among the first in England were a prolific designer of railway stations, David Mocatta, and the designer of Belgrave Square in Lon-don, Elias George Basevi, the uncle of Benjamin Disraeli. In Germany, among the first Jewish architects was Georg Friedrich Heinrich Hitzig, designer of railway stations and residential and public buildings. Other Jewish architects from Germany were the prolific design-er of railway stations, Johann Eduard Jacobsthal, and the synagogues designer Ludwig Levy. In Russia, we find such architects as synagogue and residential buildings designer Leiba Bakhman, and prolific architect of synagogues, residen-tial, and office buildings Zalman Kleinerman. In Jewish architect, and restaurateur of wooden synagogues, Josef Awin. In Austria, one of the first Jewish architects was the designer of synagogues, hospitals, schools, and residential buildings, Wilhelm Stiassny. In Hungary, there was a synagogue designer, Lipót Baumhorn. In America among the first Jewish architects who made significant contributions to local architecture was a leading Galicia, there was a noticeable architect of his time Leopold Eidlitz who designed synagogues, churches, and commercial structures. Another Jewish architect in America was a prominent ar-chitect of schools, synagogues, and com-mercial buildings, Adolph Fleischman. The list of American architects of Jewish origin includes also a synagogue archi-tect, Henry Fernbach; an architect and urban planner, Arnold W. Brunner, and an architect-engineer Dankmar Adler, to name a few. Of course, these are just the names of prominent Jewish architects.

At first and up to the end of the 19th century, Jewish architects were not at the forefront of the new trends in architecture. These newcomers sought to blend in with their elders in the profes-sion. They understood architecture as an aesthetic endeavor, which led them to a distortion of the architect's role, reducing it mainly to thedecoration of buildings in different art styles. No wonder, all studies of their work are clas-sified by the art styles, and judged by art criteria, which should be applied, most likely, only to the façade's composition and decoration of their buildings. Also, when Jewish architects started to appear on the architectural scene in the 19th century, their commissions were rather humble. However, in a short while, they took on larger, higher–profile commis-sions in the Jewish communities: syna-gogues, ritual buildings, and cemetery facilities along with such civil structures as the railway stations, and residential and public buildings. Form-wise, histor-icism was their point of departure. Later on, while designing religious buildings for Jewish clients, they started to look for a Jewish art style. That was partly analogous to other national revival movements in Europe. Jewish architects also felt obliged to indicate the Jewish identity of their buildings. But what they considered Jewish and exposed mostly in their religious architecture had completely different roots.

Jewish religious architecture in Cen-tral and Eastern Europe in the second half of the 19th century is known for a variety of synagogues with façades built in the 'Moorish Revival' art style. To-gether with other innovations in culture, this style falsely established itself perma-nently as a representative of *Jewish Ar-chitecture*, and for more than a century was associated with that architecture. To some extent, this stereotype exists even now. The 'Moorish Revival' art style is a vestige of an Orientalist interpretation of Judaism by (non-Jewish) architects. However, the first Jewish architects in the 19th century followed that tendency also. Though, by the end of the century, more comfortable in their occupation, they began to think more reflectively about architecture. Similar to the efforts of Renaissance architects to incorporate in their projects ancient Greece and Roman developments in architectural form, the architects of the late 19th century turned for inspiration to the Far East and Muslim structures, as well as to African art, reflecting the increased in-terest of the general public (read—their clients) toward all Oriental, Muslim and African. Several architectural movements and schools, which affected worldwide archi-tecture, appeared in the 20th century. Among these were Neo-Romanticism, Constructivism, Bauhaus School, Inter-national Architecture, and Post-Modern Architecture. Jewish architects played a significant role in all of them. Along with the 19th-century architects' list, there is also an endless list of Jewish architects who left a significant mark in 20th-century architecture.

Although Jews still did not have their own country to develop national architecture, Jewish architects greatly influenced Western architecture of the 19th–20th century. One of the first outstanding manifestations of their input into new 20th-century architecture was the project of Monument to the Third International in 1919, known as Tatlin's Tower (Illus. 5.4.1, 1920). Out of four participants in the project, three were Jews: Iosif Meerzon, Tevel' Shapiro, and Sofia Dymshits-Tolstaya (Illus. 5.4.2). Although it is hard to establish now the ethnicity of the team's leader Vladimir Tatlin, his last name sounds to Russian speaking ear suspiciously Jewish.

Neo-Romanticism, a short-lived movement in architecture at the beginning of the 20th century is exemplified by Jewish architect Erich Mendelsohn the author of the Einstein Tower (Illus. 5.4.3 and 5.4.4) with its dynamic, expressive design that incorporated elements of functionalism.

Jewish architect and theoretician, Moisei Ginzburg was the leader of the Constructivist movement in architecture (Illus. 5.4.5). Residential and urban designers Mikhail Barshch and Mikhail Sinyavskii were the other leading architects of constructivism (Illus. 5.4.6). Constructivists included also two outstanding Jewish architectural visionaries of the early 20th century, architects, El Lissitzky and Yakov Chernikhov (Illus. 5.4.7 and 5.4.8).[15]

Among Jewish Bauhausers were: architect and furniture designer, Marcel Breuer (Illus. 5.4.9); architect and urban planner, Arthur Korn (Illus..4.10); an architect, urban planner, and author Bruno Taut (Illus. 5.4.11), and one of the key figures in the development of modern urban planning theory and practice, Ludwig Hilberseimer (Illus.5.4.12), to name a few.

The international architecture was represented by a leading Jewish proponent of modernist architecture, Richard Neutra (Illus. 5. 4.13), and the pioneer of modern design in Brasilia Gregori Warchavchik (Illus. 5.4.14).

Jewish architects in the Post-Modern movement are exemplified by an

---

15 There were numerous practicing Jewish architects in Tsarist and Soviet Russia. Information about them can be found in the 4-volume book: Berkovich, Gary. *Reclaiming a History.* Grunberg Verlag. 2022

5.4.1. Tatlin Tower: Monument to the Third International. 1919–1920. Photo credit: public domain

5.4.2. Tatlin Tower team. From left to right: Iosif Meerzon, Tevel' Shapiro, Vladimir Tatlin, Sofia Dymshits-Tolstaya. Photo credit: public domain

5.4.3. Erich Mendelsohn. Einstein Tower. Potsdam, Germany. 1924.
Photo credit: Zain Mankani flickr.com

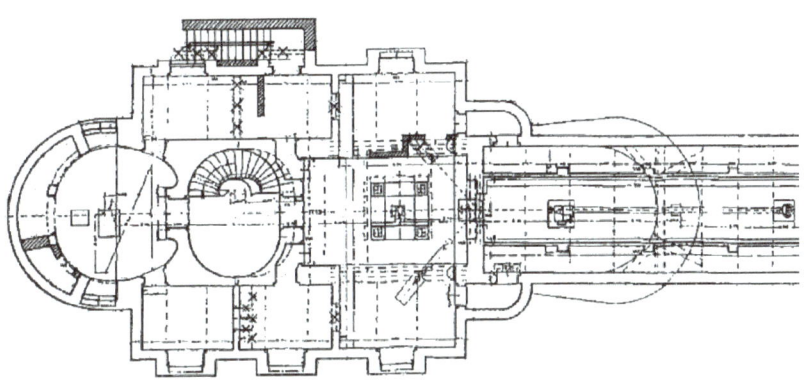

5.4.4. Erich Mendelsohn. Einstein Tower. Potsdam, Germany. 1924. Floor plan.
Photo credit: SteinKünste

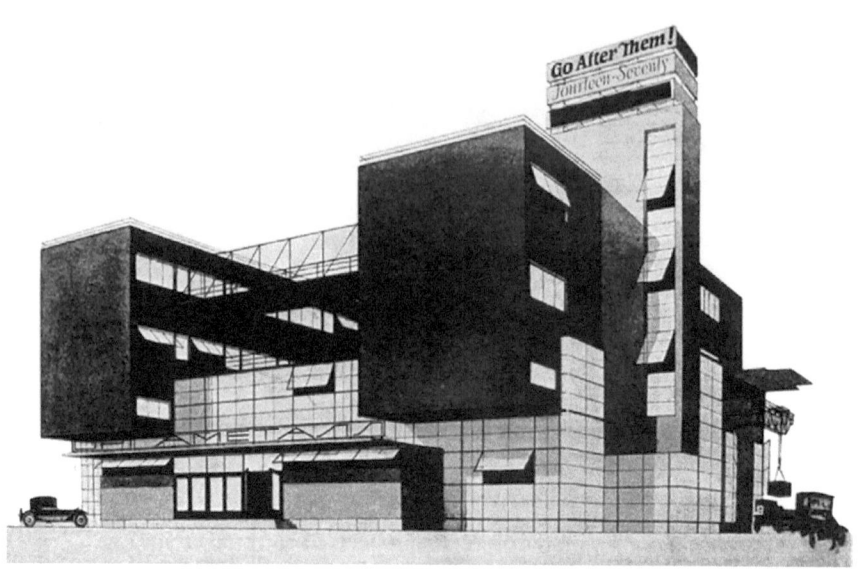

5.4.5. Moisei Ginzburg. Orgametal building competition project. Moscow. 1926. Perspective.
Photo credit: public domain

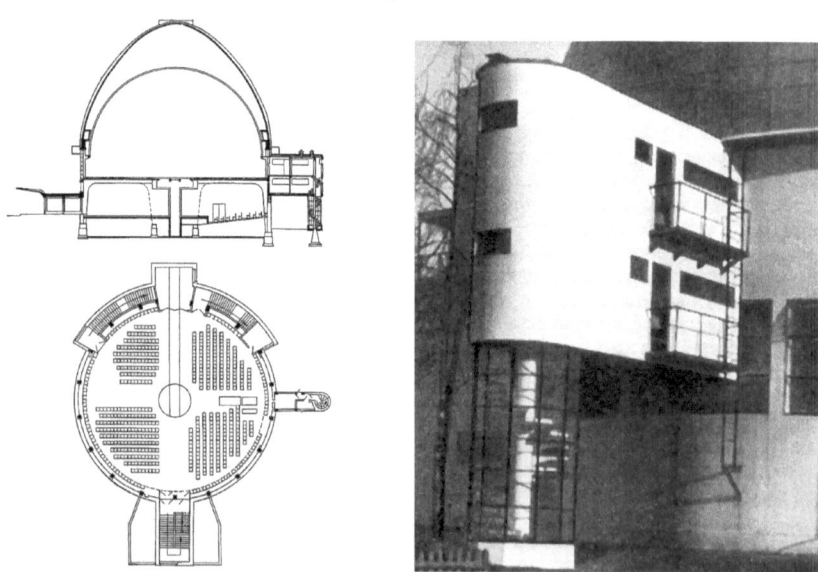

5.4.6. Mikhail Barshch and Mikhail Sinyavskii. Planetarium. Moscow. 1927-1929.
Floor plan, section and facade detail. Photo credit: public domain

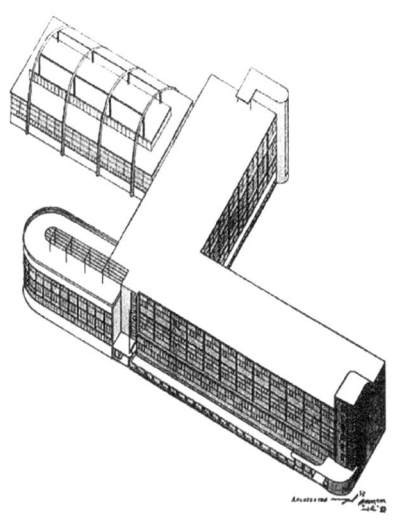

5.4.7. El Lissitzky "Ogonyok" Printhouse. Moscow, USSR. 1920s. Photo credit: public domain

5.4.8. Ya. Chernikhov. «OSA». 1932. Perspective. Photo credit: OSA, p.13

5.4.9. Marcel Breuer. Breuer House 1. New Canaan, CT. 1948. Photo credit: dwell

5.4.10. Arthur Korn. Villa Goldstein. Berliin, Germany. 1922. Photo credit: reddit.com

5.4.11. Bruno Taut. Glass Pavilion. Cologne, Germany. 1914. Photo credit: museumderdinge.de

5.4.12. Ludwig Hilberseimer. Vertical City. 1924. Photo credit: danismm.tumblr.com.com

5.4.13. Richard Neutra. Kaufmann House. Palm Springs, California. 1946.
Photo credit: claudejobin.com

5.4.14. Gregori Warchavchik. Casa Modernista, Rio de Janeiro. 1931.
Photo credit: alchetron.com

architect, urbanist, and urban planner, Moshe Safdie (Illus. 5.4.15); an author of groundbreaking designs, architect Frank Gehry (Illus. 5 4.16); and a renowned architect, artist and set designer Daniel Libeskind (Illus. 5.4.17), among numerous others.

While the number of non-Jewish architects who contributed to the foundation of contemporary architecture may be greater, the influence of Jewish architects on contemporary architecture is significant and far-reaching. Their willingness to experiment, their embrace of new ideas, and their commitment to creating meaningful spaces have left a lasting legacy on the world of architecture. To sum up, since emancipation, Jews not only greatly contributed to the Industrial Revolution and the formation of capitalism, but they also played a significant part in new artistic movements and the creation of modern architectural paradigms.

THE JEWS AND GLOBALIZATION. So far, in this chapter, we exemplified the role of Jewish clients in the development of contemporary architecture as one of its precursors. We examined also the input on contemporary architecture by various art movements and Jewish architects. Another major precursor of contemporary architecture in which the Jews played a leading role was the globalization of our planet.

There is something in Jews that eludes capture and definition and that has always set them apart. For centuries Jews had a strong sense of national identity based on belonging to a religious-ethnic-cultural group dating from ancient times. As Joseph Jacobs rightly noticed "…their creed was connected with a book and not with a city or land."[16] Century after century Jews have amazed the world with their loyalty to their religion, compassion, enterprise, imagination, and dynamism. The Jews are a people who combine humor and business acumen, a general attitude of skepticism, and a surprising vitality. Despite themselves, perhaps, Jews continue to stand out in these ways.[17] All ethnici-

16 Jacobs, Joseph. *Jewish contribution to civilization: an estimate*. The Jewish Publication Society of America. Philadelphia. 1919. P. 15.

17 See: Lynn, Richard. *The Chosen People: A Study of Jewish Intelligence and Achievement*. Washington Summit Publishers. Whitefish. MT, USA. 2011. In general, the question of the Jewish genotype, discussed already by Zeev Jabotinsky a long time ago, is a separate topic that author would not like to touch on in order not to get involved in a discussion about races, or

ties produce talented individuals marked by greater than ordinary drives to create and innovate and who have unusual capacities for concentration, persistence, and independence. Few would question that the Jews have a high percentage of such individuals among them.

In addition, being constantly in exile and persecuted by all, who are not lazy to do it, Jews at the same time are one of the most freedom–loving peoples in the world. Instead of princes, kings, and tzars, they always had only God above them. "I am not afraid of anyone, only God alone," they repeat for centuries. But what is remarkable is that a Jew never kneels, even when praying to God. This led, from generation to generation, to strengthen the spirit of freedom in their minds. Internal independence is the core of Jewish psychology. Their behavior is not dictated by the traditions of the people among whom they live. They have always been cosmopolitans.

The Czech writer and thinker Milan Kundera has noted, "Aliens everywhere and everywhere at home, lifted above national quarrels, the Jews in the twentieth century were the principal cosmopolitan, integrating element in Central Europe: they were its intellectual cement, a condensed version of its spirit, creators of its spiritual unity..."[18] Basic to this, it should be noted, is that this phenomenon has been true not only in Europe but elsewhere.

Yuri Slezkine, in the book The Jewish Century,[19] meticulously explores the historical and cultural role of the Jews in the 20th century, particularly focusing on their involvement in various intellectual, political, and cultural movements, and in general—a broad interpretation of Jewish history and its significance in the 20th century. From time immemorial, Slezkine observes, Jews have traditionally belonged to that sociological–anthropological category known as servers: the nomads and outsiders specializing in the delivery of goods and services, the enterprising minority, whom he labels Mercurians. While the peoples among whom they live, by Slezkine classification—Apollonians make up the fixed, stable, tradition–bound societies, these others are less subject

more precisely, in order to avoid accusations of racism.

---

18   See: Kundera, Milan. *Abduction of the West or The Tragedy of Central Europe (Unos západu aneb Tragédie střední Evropy)*. Gordogan 1985: 17-18. Zagreb. P. 298

19   See: Slezkine, Yuri. *The Jewish Century*. Princeton University Press. 2006.

5.4.15. Moshe Safdie, National Gallery of Canada. Ottava. Canada. 1988.
Photo credit: John Talbot/Flickr

5.4.16. Frank Gehry. The Ninewells Hospital. Dundee, Scotland. 2003.
Photo credit: Raf Makda, Heinz Architectural Center, Carnegie Museum of Art

5.4.17. Daniel Libeskind. Bundeswehr Military History Museum Addition.
Dresden, Germany. 2011. Photo credit: Eric Allen, architecturaldigest.com

to local traditions that would restrict their actions. "The difference between Apollonians and Mercurians is the crucial difference between those who raise food and those who create concepts and artifacts."[20] As Slezkine has shown in his admirable work, the Jews, as a historically marginalized group, developed a unique strategy for survival and success. He suggests that Jews have excelled in modern societies by adopting a mobile and adaptable lifestyle, often transitioning from rural to urban areas and from one profession to another. This ability to adapt and thrive in different environments allowed Jews to make significant contributions in various fields.

Slezkine explores how Jews embraced and embodied the ideals of modernity, particularly in the 20th century. He argues that Jews were at the forefront of intellectual and cultural movements, including Marxism, psychoanalysis, and Zionism. He emphasizes the Jewish role in shaping modern ideologies and social movements, highlighting their influence and impact on society. The twentieth century saw an explosion in Jewish contribution to all forms of worldwide culture, including literature, poetry, painting, music, cinematography, sculpture, and architecture. Jewish input in these areas was significant and diverse. It is well-studied and confirmed in Slezkine's research.

Among well-known Jews influential in the world's 20th-century culture are such personalities: in literature—Franz Kafka, Isaac Bashevis Singer, Primo Levi, and Saul Bellow; in poetry—Osip Mandelstam, Joseph Brodsky, Czeslaw Milosz, and Yehuda Amichai; in painting—Marc Chagall, Amedeo Modigliani, Mark Rothko, and Max Ernst; in music—Gustav Mahler, George Gershwin, Leonard Bernstein, and Irving Berlin; in cinematography—Woody Allen, Stanley Kubrick, Milos Forman, and Roman Polanski; in sculpture— Jacques Lipchitz, Louise Nevelson, Naum Gabo, and Elie Nadelman, to name a few.

Slezkine contextualizes the Jewish experience within the broader historical developments of the 20th century and examines the process of Jewish assimilation into mainstream societies. He suggests that Jews have historically sought integration into their surrounding cultures while simultaneously maintaining a distinct Jewish identity. Slezkine explores how this process unfolded differently in various regions and how it

---

20 See: Slezkine, p. 26.

affected Jewish communal life, religious practices, and cultural expression. He argues that the characteristics exhibited by Jews as a people are better adapted to life in the modern world than many other social groups and have become the chief symbol and standard of modern life worldwide. "All Mercurians represented urban arts amid rural labors, and most scriptural Mercurians emerged as the primary beneficiaries and scapegoats of the city's costly triumph, but only the Jews—the scriptural Mercurians of Europe—came to represent Mercurianism and modernity everywhere."[21] "The new market was different from old markets in that it was anonymous and socially unembedded (relatively speaking): it was exchange among strangers, with everyone trying, with varying degrees of success, to play the Jew."[22] In consequence, Slezkine terms the 20th century that saw the rise of globalization, as the *Jewish Century*.

NEW APPROACH TO ARCHITECTURE. It was triggered by the Industrial Revolution of the 19th century and the emancipation of Jews, and there was a profound difference in mentality

21 See: Slezkine, p. 43
22 Ibid. p. 46

between the architects and their Jewish clients. The architects involved then were not Jewish and did not immediately acquiesce to the demands of their Jewish clients. It was based on the fact that, as people of the Book Jews had a centuries-long tradition of debate and discussion of the Bible, the Tanakh, and had learned how to get to the abstract heart of a text or a problem. This hardly made for an easy fit with the psychology and professional training of the architects of that time, or with society's expectations of architecture.

This helps explain the importance of the modern movements regarding the appearance of Jewish architects. Now their Mercurian (using Slezkine's classification), dynamic, maverick mentality came into play. Norwegian scholar Thorleif Boman quite accurately described it as "dynamic, vigorous, passionate, and sometimes quite explosive."[23] The combination of that Jewish mentality among clients with the dynamic of new architectural trends that these clients encouraged helped architecture to overcome the static centuries-old traditions

23 See: Boman, Thorleif. *Hebrew Thought Compared with Greek*. W.W. Norton & Company, 1975.

of the Renaissance, and affected Jewish architects' approach to architecture.

Boman's contentions are cited in American architect Stanley Tigerman's book Versus, a chapter of which Postmodernism Is a Jewish Movement deals with the influence of Judaism on architecture.[24] Anticipating Slezkine by a quarter of a century on the nature of civilization as a duality of Apollonians and Mercurians, Tigerman's view of the dualism pits the ethical against the esthetic, the Hellenistic principle against the Jewish. Both Tigerman's and Slezkine's complementing each other's formulations are very important for understanding the historical role of Jews in contemporary culture and the development of contemporary architecture.

Talking about Jewish contribution to contemporary architecture, we should not underestimate the role of religion in Jewish life. Jacobs writes, "The Jews have been made what they are by the Bible, by which I mean, of course, what is usually termed the Old Testament. Their life has been dominated by its law, their feelings by its psalter, their ideals by its prophets, their outlook on life by its wisdom, and their hopes for the future by its apocalypse."[25] Referring to this subject, Tigerman makes another crucial observation: architecture, which uses images as symbols, contravenes the voice of God in the Book of Exodus, where God declares: "You shall not make a carved image for yourself nor the likeness of anything in the heavens above, or on the earth below, or in the waters under the earth. You shall not bow down to them or worship them." For Jews who would be the clients of architects and for architects raised in the theology of the Tanakh, these were not empty words. Furthermore, Jews also had imbibed with their mother's milk the strictures of kashrut, of ritual purity. One can argue that the decorative embellishment, as an aspect of the building, would not have gone down easily for those raised with Jewish moral principles.

In addition, the work of Jewish architects was inevitably influenced by the traditional interest of Jewish philosophy in the rational and abstract and the many centuries of study of the Talmud and Tanakh. That was one of the rea-

---

24 See: Tigerman, Stanley. *Versus*. New York: Rizzoli International Publications, Inc., 1982.

25 Jacobs, Joseph. *Jewish contribution to civilization: an estimate*. The Jewish Publication Society of America. Philadelphia. 1919. P. 61.

sons, why the new trends in architecture were more congenial to Jewish architects than to others when the fervor for modernism began to take hold in art and architecture in the late 19th century. Hence is the passion for the pure forms of buildings, which is found in the architecture of the early 20th century and later on.

No small role in the rethinking of the architects of that time was played by another element of the Jewish tradition of lifelong study and debate of the Tanakh: the right of each to his/her own opinion. Jewish clients freed their architects to follow this rule and not be bound by well-established traditional forms (for instance, the Neo-Classical art styles then prevalent in Europe and America). As soon as this idea took hold among the architects, it blossomed. The first examples were factories and other industrial structures. But by the middle of the 19th century, there began to appear non–industrial structures, which reflected the new rational approach to architecture and the architect's place in the building process. The *paxtons, sullivans, wrights* and *gaudis*, quickly made their presence felt in the form of landmark creations of a highly individualistic nature. Industrial architecture had its elevators, power stations, factories, railway depots, and bridges; non-industrial architecture had its exhibition halls, private residences, skyscrapers, stores, and theaters. The transition was painful and protracted, stretching out over more than a century. Still, the gradual rejection of the primacy of Renaissance forms and ideas was clear even as early as the latter half of the 19th century with the Arts and Crafts movement. Formal explorations were underway in many directions. Often this manifested itself in the mimicking of various vernacular styles of various epochs. Sometimes architects chose to experiment within the bounds of traditional classic styles but eschew strict conformity (for example, by way of eclecticism, a mixing of historical styles, as Gaudi in Europe, and McKim-Mead in the United States). Japanese architecture, then only recently discovered by Europe, was very influential as well.

Slezkine noticed an interesting phenomenon of the 20th century: it was not the Jews who disappeared into the cultures of the surrounding nations, but the surrounding nations adopted the Jewish culture, "...first in Europe and then elsewhere, [they] had to become more like the Jews: urban, mobile, literate, mentally nimble, occupationally flexible, and surrounded by aliens (and thus keen on cleanliness, unmanliness, and creative dietary taboos)."[26] It is echoed by Renato Rizzi, who asserts "...that modernism is incomprehensible without a proper understanding of the Jewish contribution to modernity. Although the Code Napoléon started Jewish emancipation by the end of the 18th century, its impact on architecture and city development became visible only a century later peaking in modernism. Modernity and modernism offered mankind experiences that were familiar to the Jews during their history: losing physical roots, living scattered, fragmentation, exclusion, multiple cultural belonging."[27]

The global civilization, which adopted Jewish culture, has been formed. The centuries-old branched and active Jewish diaspora served as the nucleus of the embryo of modern globalization. Jewish diaspora contributed greatly to its establishment and development.

Our planet's globalization contributed to the unity of the Jewish nation and the fusion of the cultures of separate disparate Jewish enclaves. At the same time, this globalization is a sign of global recognition of the centuries-long Jewish traditions.

As a derivative of this era, a part of this Jewish culture was and is architecture. Accordingly, this architecture, the architecture of global civilization that took shape in the 20th century, has replaced national architectures. The era of global civilization, the *Jewish Century*, has given rise to the era of global *Jewish Architecture*. This will form the subject of our next chapter.

---

26 See: Slezkine, Yuri. *The Jewish Century*. Princeton University Press. 2006. P. 46

27 Quoted from: Klein, Rudolf. 'Jewish Architecture' of the late 20th century. IZGRADNJA 66 (2012) 3–4, 16–31. Academia.edu. 2012. P. 14

Chapter 6. *Jewish Architecture*

To explore *Jewish Architecture*, we have devoted the preceding chapters to a comprehensive discussion of key topics related to it. Specifically, we have delved into various aspects of architecture, both in its general sense and as an integral part of national cultures. Our exploration included an analysis of the Jewish impact on the architecture of host countries and the influential role of Jewish clients in the evolution of contemporary architecture. Furthermore, we have examined the Jewish contribution to the development of current architectural typology and form creation, along with the influence of Jewish architects on globalization and their pivotal role in shaping contemporary architecture.

Additionally, our discussion has touched upon several architectural paradigms that emerged during the nineteenth century in Europe and America. As observed, these paradigms were rooted in the concept of architecture as a component of art. In the latter part of the nineteenth century, as we have explored, the architectural paradigm underwent its transformation under the influence of various art movements such as Arts and Crafts, Art Nouveau, and others. These movements were themselves significantly shaped by the societal changes brought about by the Industrial Revolution.

Despite the influences of these art movements, our observation revealed that the nineteenth-century architectural paradigms originated from a strong inclination towards reviving various art styles in architecture, including Neoclassical, Greek, Gothic, and others.

As the twentieth century unfolded, a new, contemporary architectural paradigm began to take shape, continually evolving in response to emerging technologies and cultural shifts. This paradigm encompasses the development of innovative building types, a functional approach to design, and often adopts a minimalist aesthetic. This minimalist perspective places a strong emphasis on clean lines, simple forms, and a focus on essential elements. Notably, the defining characteristic of this contemporary architectural paradigm is its global scope.

As our exploration revealed, Jews have played a pivotal role in shaping the modern architectural paradigm. We delved into the multifaceted ways in which the Jewish diaspora, starting in the nineteenth century, has left a lasting impact on modern architecture. Throughout the first half of that century and beyond, Jews actively participated as clients, commissioners, and financiers, contributing to the emergence of innovative architectural structures and urban planning. By the close of the nineteenth century and in subsequent years, they assumed a central role in nurturing emerging artistic movements and providing financial support for the exploration of inventive artistic forms, significantly contributing to the development of groundbreaking architectural movements.

In the subsequent phases of their influence on the contemporary architectural paradigm, Jews rose to prominence as key figures within avant-garde movements in art and architecture during the twentieth century. Finally, in the late twentieth and early 21st centuries, Jews continued to exert a profound influence on the global landscape and its architecture.

As we discussed, the architecture of any nation is a product of its development within its territory. However, the increasing globalization of our planet has resulted in the internationalization of national architectures. Consequently, the concept of distinct national architectures has started to lose its clarity. With the insights gathered from our studies and discussions in earlier chapters, we can now direct our attention to this phenomenon and explore how it has given rise to the distinct entity of *Jewish Architecture*.

CURRENT DEFINITIONS. The term '*Jewish Architecture*' is widely used in both general and scholarly discourse, encompassing a diverse range of interpretations. One prevalent definition associated it with buildings designed by architects of the Jewish diaspora. Architects such as Leopold Eidlitz, Dankmar Adler, Emery Roth, Arnold W. Brunner, Lipót Baumhorn, Ludwig Levy, Wilhelm Stiassny, and others are often cited as examples, particularly for their iconic Jewish projects. It is worth noting, however, that we do not categorize, for example, as German architecture, the works of German architects, designed for specific German use or German clients outside of Germany. Similarly, the works of architects from the Korean or Chinese diaspora in countries such as Brazil, South Africa, Argentina, or the United States—whether residential, public, industrial, or religious—aren't classified as Korean or Chinese architecture. Instead, they are part of the host nations' architecture. This observation holds true for architects of any diaspora.

But even if we do try to recognize the works of Jewish architects as *Jewish Architecture*, there is not much in common in the buildings designed by them. As Paul Goldberger noticed, "… there is plenty of architecture produced by Jewish architects and much of it is very good, some of it even great. But the things that make it good are not necessarily Jewish things, and I do not see that there are common themes running through buildings by Jewish architects. Richard Meier is not like Frank Gehry who is not like Robert Stern who is not like Peter Eisenman, to name four architects of Jewish origin." There is one commonality in contemporary buildings by Jewish architects: they all follow general trends of local and global architecture.

At times, buildings designed with a distinctively Jewish purpose, such as religious and public structures, are often cited as examples of *Jewish Architecture*.[1] Synagogues and Jewish community centers are frequently viewed in this context. For instance, the Jerusalem Synagogue in Prague, designed by architect Wilhelm Stiassny (Illus. 6.1.1), as well as other synagogues by Jewish architect Ludwig Levy in France or Germany (Illus. 6.1.2), are commonly referenced as notable examples of *Jewish Architecture*. Additionally, Holocaust memorials and museums, irrespective of their location, are commonly associated with *Jewish Architecture*.

However, structures of a similar nature serving other nationalities' diasporas are typically categorized as part of the host country's architecture. Public or religious buildings representing Armenian, Greek, Bulgarian, and other nationalities in the USA, such as churches commissioned by the Korean diaspora in America (Illus. 6.1.3), are all considered components of American ar-

---

1 Or, as Wikipedia authors put it, it is "the architecture of Jewish religious buildings and other buildings that either incorporate Jewish elements in their design or are used by Jewish communities." See: https://en.wikipedia.org/wiki/Jewish_architecture.

6.1.1. Wilhelm Stiassny. Jerusalem synagogue. Prague, Czech Republic. 1906. Photo credit: govisity.com

6.1.2. Ludwig Levy. Synagogue in Strasbourg, France. 1898. Photo credit: Bibliotheque et universitaire de Strasbourg

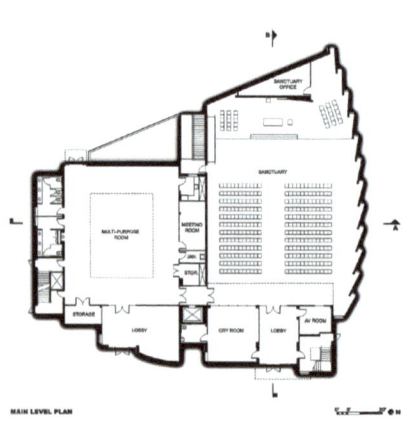

6.1.3. Korean Presbyterian Church. Oakland, NJ. USA. 2013. Floor plan. Photo credit: Arcari+Iovino Architects

chitecture. Similarly, a Buddhist temple in Europe or America, even if incorporating Indian or Chinese architectural elements, would not usually be referred to as an example of Indian architecture. Likewise, a museum dedicated to the Ukrainian Holodomor, adorned with architectural elements from the Ukrainian so-called Baroque architecture period, would not be deemed Ukrainian architecture if located outside of Ukraine.

As the architecture of any nation can be defined as the totality of structures developed on that nation's land, reflecting its character, aesthetic values, climate, local materials, and construction methods, the architecture of the Jewish nation is often defined as structures built for or by Jews. This raises questions about the unequal approach to defining *Jewish Architecture* compared to the architecture of other nations, prompting scrutiny of its scientific validity and consistency.

'JEWISH APPEARANCE.' When it comes to synagogues, an explanation for this discrepancy in defining *Jewish Architecture* can be found in what some people refer to as the 'Jewish appearance' of these structures. This particularly applies to synagogue buildings from the nineteenth and early twentieth centuries, when architecture was universally regarded as an art form, and evaluated and classified based on artistic criteria.

In the realm of art, the concept of style, which primarily pertains to the sculptural aspect of architecture, became a major defining point in the field, especially since the Renaissance. However, the sculptural facet of architecture has always been a controversial aspect of Jewish tradition. This was one of the reasons why synagogue buildings, particularly in small shtetls, were often constructed without elaborate decorations, resembling local housing structures. Only in larger towns, influenced by the cultures of host countries, did synagogues adopt special forms and decorations characteristic of local architecture. This trend persisted during the Renaissance and beyond. In the nineteenth century, there was a notable shift with the emergence of reform synagogues. These synagogues incorporated various derivatives of the Renaissance in their façade decorations. One notable offshoot, although based rather on Gothic and medieval Muslim architectural forms, was the so-called 'Moorish Revival.'

At the beginning of the nineteenth century, there were no Jewish architects. Consequently, non-Jewish architects were responsible for carrying out Jewish commissions, particularly for synagogue construction. These architects were fascinated by the intricate decorative elements found in medieval Spanish buildings, influenced by Muslim architecture from that period, commonly known as the 'Moorish style.' Thus, in early nineteenth-century Europe, non-Jewish architects developed a *pseudo-Jewish Architecture* for European synagogues characterized by a pseudo-Jewish artistic style known as the 'Moorish Revival' (Illus. 6.1.4 and 6.1.5).[2] This style incorporated features such as domes, horseshoe arches, and elaborate sculptural details reminiscent of the Spanish period of Islamic architecture.

The adoption of the 'Moorish Revival' artistic style for synagogues reflected the perception of non-Jewish architects that Judaism was inherently Oriental. Consequently, synagogues designed in the 'Moorish Revival' art style emerged.

6.1.4 Synagogue. Ingenheim. Germany.1832. Photo credit: allemania-judaica.de

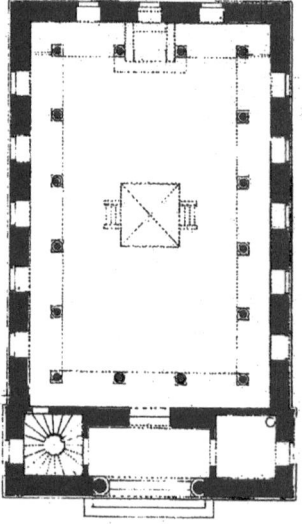

6.1.5. Synagogue. Ingenheim. Germany. 1832. Floor plan. Photo credit: allemania-judaica.de

---

2 It was introduced in the Ingenheim synagogue (1832) by German architect Friedrich von Gartner (1791–1847) and became well known after it appeared in the Dresden synagogue (1838–1840) by another German architect Gottfried Semper (1803–1879).

This art style was accepted by the Jewish diaspora and became associated with Jewish structures. Paul Goldberger aptly described this phenomenon when he stated, "...since Moorish architecture has elements of the Near East and some elements of the Mediterranean cultures, it could even be said to have a logical connection to Jewish origins, and with the absence of any stronger association to trump this one, it became a kind of quasi-synagogue style, at least by default."[3] However, it is important to note that the adoption of the 'Moorish Revival' style for synagogues may also have been influenced by anti-Semitic sentiments, as it accentuated the foreign origins of Jews.

During the nineteenth century, when 'Moorish Revival' synagogues were constructed, Jews had only recently secured equal rights alongside other peoples. These diaspora Jews, who had made significant contributions to the economies and cultures of their host nations, sought to establish their distinct national identity in architecture—a unique *Jewish Architecture*. Given that architecture was widely regarded as an art form during this period, Jews adopted the artificially created art style of 'Moorish Revival' and considered it their architectural language.

The integration of 'Moorish Revival' details on synagogue façades, later extending to other building types, proved to be a convenient innovation. This pseudo-Jewish sculptural element of architecture has misled many, including professionals. The prevalence of 'Moorish Revival' details can also be attributed to the fact that Jews lacked a Jewish state where a distinctive Jewish architectural language could develop. The architectural language of ancient Hebrew architecture had been obliterated by the Romans, and a new one could not emerge until the Jews restored their state.

While the 'Moorish Revival Style' synagogues were initially constructed for the reformist segment of emancipated Sephardic Jews in the diaspora, these buildings played a significant role in the history of Jews as representatives of *Jewish Architecture* throughout the modern diaspora. However, by essentially representing the architectural epoch of Medieval Islam, they created a false Jewish identity in architecture.

---

3 See: Goldberger, Paul. Is there a *Jewish Architecture?* A lecture at the Jewish Center of the Hamptons. August 26, 2011. http://www.paulgoldberger.com/lectures/is-there-a-jewish-architecture/

Simultaneously with the introduction of decorative elements from the 'Moorish Revival Style,' the large synagogues of that time, built by affluent Jews embracing Reform Judaism, began to increasingly resemble contemporary churches. Instead of the bimah and reading table being situated in the center of the room with seating arranged around it, they adopted an oblong, often three-aisled plan. The bimah was shifted from the center of the sanctuary to the eastern wall where the Ark was located, an organ was included, and rose windows were added to the façade, among other features. All these alterations represented a significant departure from the original tenets of Judaism.

As a result, not only various synagogues were erected in Central and Eastern Europe in the second half of the nineteenth century, but other building types such as cemetery structures and even residential buildings are known for façades in the 'Moorish Revival' mode as well. Since this practice migrated to many countries, it established itself permanently as a representative of *Jewish Architecture*. It should be noted that synagogues with 'Moorish Revival Style' façades differed from synagogues with, for example, Classical art style façades only in their appearance. This practice followed a similar approach in any other types of buildings of the nineteenth century, which differ only in appearance. In general, the development of the typology of urban dwellings in Europe from the fourteenth century to the eighteenth century shows that it mainly changed its shell. It was only the sculptural component of its architecture that was changing.

For over a century, the 'Moorish Revival Style' has been linked to *Jewish Architecture*. However, since this art style is essentially an Orientalist interpretation of Judaism by non-Jewish architects of the nineteenth century (given the absence of Jewish architects at that time), buildings featuring 'Moorish Revival' decorative elements, despite their significant influence, cannot be accurately labeled as *Jewish Architecture*.

Moreover, 'The Moorish Revival' did not evolve as a grassroots movement among architects; rather, it was imposed from above. It emerged at the behest of influential individuals within Jewish elite circles, often referred to as 'enlightened circles.' An illustrative example described by Sergey Kravtsov is indicative: «The Neoclassicist synagogue called 'Deutsch-israelitisches Bethhaus'

(German-Israelite House of Prayer) reveals changes undergone by Galician Judaism. Its building committee, which was comprised of wealthy maskilim, invited R. Abraham Kohn (1807–1848), a rigorous adherent of Reform, Jewish Enlightenment, and German assimilation to officiate in the city. Favored within enlightened circles, he was hated by both Hasidim and Mitnagdim as 'German, ignorant, and non-kosher.' The committee proclaimed its intention to model the new synagogue on those of Vienna and Prague."[4]

Acknowledging the significant role played by 'Moorish Revival' in identifying Jewish buildings, it is crucial to note that, even if one were to consider it *Jewish Architecture*, even from the most liberal point of view, this Medieval art style pertains exclusively to one Jewish group in the diaspora—the Sephardim. 'Moorish Revival' architecture is foreign to Ashkenazic, Mizrahi, and Ethiopian Jews; Georgian and Mountain Jews from the Caucasus; Indian Jews, including the Malabar Yehuddim (Cochin Jews), Bene Israel, Bnei Menashe, and Bene Ephraim; the Romaniotes of Greece; the ancient Italian Jewish community; the Teimanim from Yemen; various African Jews, notably the Beta Israel of Ethiopia; the Bukharan Jews of Central Asia; and Chinese Jews, particularly the Kaifeng Jews.

The popularity of the 'Moorish Revival' declined in the twentieth century, and today, buildings adorned with this artistic style are museum-type heritage. 'Moorish Revival' structures as well as structures of other so-called architectural styles are museum artifacts and, in this sense, they are worthy of study, like any other artifacts. Nevertheless, due to the enduring familiarity and acceptance of 'Moorish Revival' as a representation of Jewish national architecture, many in-dividuals, both Jewish and non-Jewish, maintain this perspective. It is crucial, however, to emphasize that considering 'Moorish Revival' or structures with a 'Jewish appearance' as *Jewish Architecture* should not be endorsed solely based on popular beliefs, as historical misconcep-tions have persisted for centuries, such as the notion of a flat Earth or the Sun revolving around it.

GLOBAL *JEWISH ARCHITECTURE*. While examining various interpretations of the concept of *Jewish*

---

[4] See: Kravtsov, Sergey R. *Jewish Identities in Synagogue Architecture of Galicia and Bukovina*. Arts Judaica: The Bar-Ilan Journal of Jewish Art, 6 (2020).

Architecture, it becomes apparent that it neither exclusively represents buildings for the Jews nor by the Jews, and the notion of a distinct 'Jewish appearance' is fiction. It leads to the assertion that, in the contemporary world, *Jewish Architecture* may not exist at all. This perspective is echoed by writers like Rudolf Klein, who contends that "The expression '*Jewish Architecture*' is conditional, philosophically incorrect."[5] Paul Goldberger similarly posits that "Just as there are plenty of great Jewish artists but not any particularly meaningful school of Jewish art, there are plenty of great Jewish architects but not anything truly meaningful that we can say about what constitutes *Jewish Architecture*."[6] Probably, both authors are right, but only if we consider architecture as a part of art. The same applies to the viewpoint of other essayists, who, looking at certain examples of Israeli architecture as supposedly Jewish, reject it as being *Jewish Architecture*. The reason for this is that interpreting buildings' architecture from an aesthetic point of view, they do not find any purely Jewish stylistic elements in it.[7]

Attempts to establish a Jewish national architecture in Palestine by adopting stylistic features of Middle Eastern vernacular architecture were made in the early twentieth century.[8] Alas, this led nowhere. All efforts to synthesize Jewish national architecture by using various stylistic components have failed. And indeed, there is no *Jewish Architecture* on Earth if we understand architecture as a purely aesthetic endeavor.

However, if we view architecture in its fundamental sense—as the creation and organization of space and a form for human activity—attempts to create such architecture did find a place in Palestine in the mid–1930s in the works of former members of the Bauhaus that existed from 1919 to 1933 in Weimar, Germany, and was instrumental in generating and publicizing the ideas of Modern design in the twentieth century. Bauhaus architects, who escaped Nazis

---

5 See Klein, Rudolf. *Jewish Architecture of the late twentieth century*. Izgradnja 66 (2012) 3–4, 16–31. Academia.edu. 2012. P. 2

6 See: Goldberger, Paul. Is there a *Jewish Architecture*? A lecture at the Jewish Center of the Hamptons. August 26, 2011. http://www.paulgoldberger.com/lectures/is-there-a-jewish-architecture/

7 For instance, the Israeli architect and publicist Gerard Neumann. See: http://www.jpost.com/Opinion/No-such-thing-as-Jewish-architecture-402192.

8 e. g. Alexander Baerwald (1877–1930)

and settled in the Eretz Yisrael, focused on the functionality of buildings and the plasticity of their volumetric solutions, siting, and climactic conditions. And they eschewed decorative elements of architecture (Illus. 6. 2.1, 6.2.2, 6.2.3, and 6.2.4). Notable progress was achieved, culminating in the iconic White City in Tel Aviv, recognized as a UNESCO World Heritage Site that was among the first signs of both Israeli and global modern architecture.[9]

In essence, the Jewish nation lacks a distinctive national architecture comparable to other nations. Instead, Jewish vernacular architecture incorporates elements from the host nations. Resounding this sentiment, Steven Fine notes that the vernacular architecture of Jews "is always derivative of local styles and patterns, and responds to the needs of local minority communities."[10] Whether in Arab countries, Siberia, Poland, Germany, Spain, or other diaspora locations, Jewish houses bear a resemblance to those of their indigenous

6.2.1. White City. Tel Aviv, Israel. 1930s
Photo by author.

6.2.2. Haller, Zeev. Ehrlich House. Tel Aviv. Israel. 1933.
Photo credit: The White City Center

---

9 See: Cohen, Nahoum. *Bauhaus Tel Aviv*. B T Batsford, London, 2003.

10 See: Fine, Steven. *Writing a history of Jewish Architecture*;

https://www.khanacademy.org/humanities/ap-art-history/introduction-cultures-religions-apah/judaism-apah/a/writing-a-history-of-jewish-architecture

6.2.3. White City. Tel Aviv, Israel. 1930s
Photo by author

6.2.4. Ze'ev Rechter. Engel House.
Tel Aviv, Israel. 1934.
Photo credit: The White City Center

neighbors, emphasizing a pervasive lack of distinctiveness. The same applies to any other Jewish buildings, including places of worship.

Like any other nationality, Jews have been involved in architecture from the deepest antiquity. Among the achievements of ancient *Jewish Architecture* were palace structures, particularly from the time of Herod, both Temples that stood in Jerusalem, city walls, bridges, aqueducts, and viaducts. However, for almost 2,000 years, the Jewish people did not produce any ethnically *Jewish Architecture*, and unfortunately, we cannot find traces of it in ancient ruins.

Antique architecture is mostly known through the remnants of temples. The ancient Greeks and Romans, who worshipped many gods, had numerous temples, many of which have survived in some form. In contrast, ancient Israel, with its monotheistic belief in one God, had only one temple, and the Romans left almost nothing of it after conquering Jewish land. Not too much is remaining to study. Ancient Rome actively sought to erase the memory of everything connected with Jewish culture, and the work of Jewish architects in their land was nearly entirely demolished. Since then, the Jews did not have their own country, and the architecture of houses and religious buildings of Jews reflected the culture of the host nations, even in the Jewish land, which was taken from them for almost two millennia.

Furthermore, during their occupation of the territory of Israel, the Romans imposed their own culture, leading to the loss of Jewish architectural traditions, typology, and stylistic elements. This is evident in the surviving remains of synagogues with their sprinklings of Roman architectural details (Illus. 6.3.1). Excavations of ancient Jewish sites provide only a partial understanding of the nature of urban settlements.

Due to the destruction of the Jewish state, original *Jewish Architecture*, and Jewish architectural traditions could not progress naturally. For centuries, Jews neither created nor could create a distinctively *Jewish Architecture*. After the destruction of the Jewish state in the first century C.E. and the dispersal of Jews throughout the world, they lacked a country to develop Jewish national architecture for the next 18 centuries.

In the Middle Ages, all land in Europe, except that of the Catholic Church, was owned by powerful feudal

6.3.1. Kfar Nakhum Synagogue.
4th-5th century. Israel.
Photo by author

lords. They constructed palaces and castles and financed the construction of buildings for the church. All construction, whether in the cities or outside them, was subject to the approval of the lords. From time to time, Jews also were allowed to build—homes, shops, workshops, and synagogues. However, as outsiders, they were subject to constantly changing rules, which might include exile from the country in which they found themselves. Since Jews did not have a right to own land in Europe until the late eighteenth century, such structures as were built went up on leased land and only by special permission, the so-called privileges. But these buildings might be confiscated at any time. Jews who built did so only quasi-legally. As a rule, the activities open to Jews were limited to the areas of finance (money-lending), trade, and minor crafts, but architecture as an occupation was never among the professions open to Jews. Additionally, there was no secular education for Jews at all. A similar pattern persisted even during more enlightened times when the land transitioned into the possession of the aristocrats of medieval times, the gentry.

All changed when Jews achieved equal rights and actively engaged in society's culture. As outlined in the previous chapter, modern international architecture emerged from significant developments in Western societies and a major reassessment of aesthetics triggered by the Industrial Revolution. Jews not only initiated but also played a leading role in this transformation. The fundamentals of contemporary Western architecture nurtured and supported by Jews are characterized by a rationalistic mindset, functionalism, and purity of form. They are are reflective of traditional Jewish thinking and ultimately triumphed. This legacy represents the contribution of emancipated Jews to the architecture of Western civilization.

Contemporary architecture thus stands as one of the remarkable outcomes of Jewish emancipation. Fueled by the Jewish spirit of enterprise, with an inherent resistance to conventionality, it has introduced an entirely new lexicon of contemporary architecture to the world. Adolf Loos, a pioneer and theorist of twentieth-century contemporary architecture, noted in his early twentieth-century essay "Die Emanzipation des Judenthums" that "behind the search for a modernist [architectural] vocabulary were, first of all, emancipated Jews."[11] This vocabulary, rooted in new structures, technologies, and forms, served as the foundation for emerging architecture. Given its cosmopolitanism, dynamism, independence from local traditions and historicism, universal spirit, and those who founded, financed, and developed it, it can scarcely be labeled anything other than *Jewish Architecture*.

Indeed, European civilization often perceived it as such. In the 1890s, French society strongly reacted to the new Art Nouveau trend by promptly

---

11 See: Loos, Adolf, *Die Emanzipation des Judenthums*, in: Die Schriften 1897–1900, ed. A. Opel, Wien, 1997

labeling it *Jewish Architecture*. By the mid-twentieth century, renowned Italian architect Bruno Zevi described the connection as unmistakable. He even formulated his conception of *Jewish Architecture* as non-conforming and constantly experimental.

Each human civilization, in every epoch of its development, gives rise to its unique culture, and an invariable component of this culture is its architecture. From ancient civilizations such as the Egyptian, Mesopotamian, ancient Greek, and ancient Roman eras to the European Middle Ages, the Renaissance, and the Industrial Revolution, including the different evolution eras of Japan, China, India, and the countries of Central Asia and the Middle East, each has contributed to its architecture. Continuing this historical trajectory, the era of Mercury, as per Slezkine's terminology, led to the emergence of what is termed the architecture of Mercury. Slezkine rightly argues that one of the significant outcomes of globalization was the formation of a Jewish-influenced global society, leading him to coin the term "the Jewish Century" for the twentieth century. Following this reasoning, the Jewish Century consequently gave rise to what we now recognize as *Jewish Architecture*.

Clearly defined by the end of the nineteenth century and firmly established in the twentieth, *Jewish Architecture* did not evolve as a national architecture. It has no borders.

It's essential to highlight that the defining features of contemporary global *Jewish Architecture* took shape during the nineteenth and twentieth centuries, a period when the clientele for architecture expanded beyond the original Jewish initiators, and Jews constituted only a small fraction of architects and clients. Despite a decline in the proportion of Jewish capital and the influence of Jewish clients over the last century, *Jewish Architecture* has, paradoxically, spread worldwide.

As mentioned earlier, this transformation began with the demand for new building types. By the end of the nineteenth century, the introduction of innovative building materials (reinforced concrete, iron, steel, glass) and technologies triggered a stylistic revolution as well. This revolution spawned a diverse range of twentieth-century architectural movements, including Art Nouveau, Functionalism, Constructivism, Art Deco, International Style, Modernism,

Post-Modernism, Deconstructivism, and Hi-Tech. Collectively, these movements reflected the global acceptance of the core tenets of *Jewish Architecture*: functionalism, rationalism, internationalism replacing national and ethnic influences, a rejection of historical art styles, and complete freedom in form creation.

It's important to acknowledge that, while generalizations help trace the overall trend, exceptions exist. Not all customers of Western architecture and modern Western architects were Jews, and conversely, some Jewish customers and architects did not adhere to the general trend.

It is reasonable to suggest that a substantial portion of the current global architecture—skyscrapers, theaters, stadiums, arenas, and airport terminals, indistinguishable whether in London, Chicago, or Shanghai— largely owes its origin and development to Jews. Beyond financial contributions over the past two centuries, Jews have infused their worldview, energy, and disregard for local customs into the architecture of our contemporary era.

Lorenzo de Medici (15th century), Popes Leo X and Paul III (15th-16th century), Cardinal Borghese (from 1605, Pope Paul V), and Popes Innocent X and Alexander VII (the latter three spanning the 16th and 17th centuries) were not architects themselves. However, as patrons of Florentine (and Italian, in general) architects, they transformed Western architecture from being the art of building to building the art. Similarly, Jewish patrons of architects at the turn of the 19th and 20th centuries played a pivotal role in reinstating the essence of architecture and returned architecture to the art of building habitat.

It could be asserted that the architecture of today is, to a significant extent, the result of Jewish influence, even though many prominent practitioners of *Jewish Architecture*, such as Tadao Ando, Norman Foster, Zaha Hadid, Rem Koolhaas, Renzo Piano, and others, are not Jewish. Numerous buildings representing *Jewish Architecture* serve specific Jewish purposes also. Noteworthy examples include the North Shore Congregation Israel synagogue in Glencoe, IL, USA (Illus. 6.3.2 and 6.3.3), designed by Japanese-origin American architect Minoru Yamasaki. Other synagogues, designed by Jewish architects Percival Goodman (Illus. 6.3.4 and 6.3.5) and Sidney Eisenshtat (Illus. 6.3.6 and 6.3.7), contribute to the diverse landscape of *Jewish Architecture*.

6.3.2. Minoru Yamasaki. Synagogue. Glencoe IL. USA. 1964. Photo by author

6.3.3. Minoru Yamasaki. Synagogue. Glencoe IL. USA. 1964. Interior. Photo by author

6.3.4. Percival Goodman. Congregation Beth Israel. Lebanon, Pennsylvania, USA. 1959. Street vew. Photo credit: Wang Chiu-Hwa

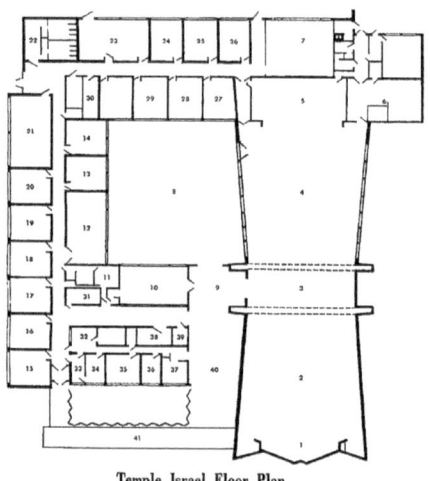

Temple Israel Floor Plan

The above is a floor plan of the new Temple Israel. 1. Ark and Choir; 2. Main Sanctuary; 3. Main Lounge; 4. Social Hall; 5. Stage; 6. Kitchen; 7. Storage; 8. Shulhof; 9. Lobby; 10. Chapel; 11. Bride's Room; 12. Library; 13-20. School Rooms; 21. Youth Lounge; 22. Toilets; 23-29. School Rooms; 30. Supply Rooms; 31. Toilets; 32-37. Offices; 38. Cloak Room; 39. Gift Shop; 40. Foyer; 41. Covered Walk.

6.3.5. Percival Goodman. Congregation Beth Israel. Philadelphia, Pennsylvania, USA. 1959. Floor plan. Photo credit: Wang Chiu-Hwa

6.3.6. Sidney Eizenshtat. B'nai Zion synagogue. El Paso, Texas. 1983.
Photo credit: 360.anmuseum.org.il

6.3.7. Sidney Eizenshtat. Temple Mount Sinai synagogue. El Paso, Texas. 1961.
Photo credit: postcard

Examples of *Jewish Architecture* include also the Jubilee Church in Rome, Italy (Illus. 6.3.8), which was designed by Jewish architect Richard Meier, and buildings by Chinese-origin architect I. M. Pei in America and Europe (Illus. 6.3.9 and 6.3.10). Given that *Jewish Architecture* is not confined to a single nation but is global in scope, it encompasses numerous structures created in different countries by foreign architects. For instance, there are buildings in Hong Kong by English architects Norman Foster (Illus. 6.3.11) and Zaha Hadid 6.3.12), in France and the USA by Spanish architects (of Jewish origin), respectively, Ricardo Bofill (Illus. 6.3.13) and Santiago Calatrava (Illus. 6.3.14 and 6.3.15). Chinese buildings by French architect Paul Andreu (Illus. 6.3.16 and 6.3.17), and structures by American architect César Pelli Levi in Kuala Lumpur, Malaysia, and Bilbao, Spain (Illus. 6.3.18 and 6.3.19), along with American buildings by Swiss architect Mario Botta (Illus. 6.3.20), are just a few examples.

While most of the exponents of what we are considering *Jewish Architecture* were not Jewish, the true founders and principal driving force in it were the Jewish entrepreneurs who commissioned and inspired this architecture. It was their child.

As in economics, finance, and commerce, where Jews constantly searched for free unexplored by others and therefore not occupied by any areas of application of their efforts, so in architecture, they searched for the most promising niches for innovation that no one had tried.

Just as noted by Rudolf Klein, the Jews "...have been formulating/amplifying/summarizing general tendencies of architecture, as they have been acting—often inspired by the Jewish heritage—in many other fields: religion, philosophy, physics, music and others (Jesus Christ, Maimonides, Baruch Spinoza, Karl Marx, Henry Bergson, Emanuel Levinas, Jacques Derrida, Albert Einstein, Ilya Prigogine, Arnold Schoenberg, Alfred Schnittke, György Ligeti, for instance)."[12]

Contrary to the early twentieth century when *Jewish Architecture* emerged, the later part of the twentieth and early 21st centuries saw a significant presence of Jews among prominent architects. Figures such as Richard Neutra, Moisei

12 See: Klein, Rudolf. *'Jewish Architecture' of the late twentieth century*. IZGRADNJA 66 (2012) 3–4, 16–31. Academia.edu. 2012. P. 2

6.3.8. Richard Meier. Jubilee Church. Rome, Italy. 2003. Street view. Photo by author

6.3.9. I.M.Pei. Bank of China. Hong Kong. 1990. Photo by author

6.3.10. I.M.Pei. National Gallery of Art. Washington, DC, USA. 1978.
Photo credit: beckchris.wordpress.com

6.3.11. Norman Foster. Airport. Hong Kong. 1998. Photo by autor

6.3.12. Zaha Hadid. Aliyev Center. Baku, Azerbaijan. 2012. Photo by author

6.3.13. Ricardo Bofill. Arcades du Lac, France. Ricardo Bofill. 1982.
Photo credit: Ricardo Bofill

6.3.14. Santiago Calatrava. Art museum. Milwaukee WI, USA. 2015. Street view.
Photo by author.

6.3.15. Santiago Calatrava. Art museum. Milwaukee WI, USA. 2015. Interior.
Photo by author

6.3.16. Paul Andreu. National Grand Theater of China. Beijing, China. 2007. Street view.
Photo by author

6.3.17. Paul Andreu. National Grand Theater of China. Beijing, China. 2007. Interior.
Photo by author

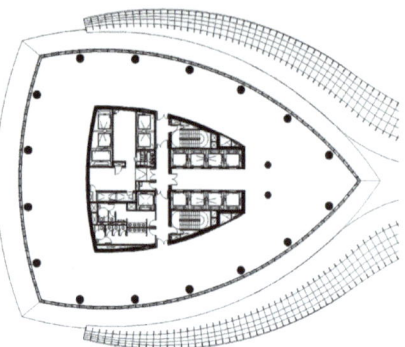

6.3.18. Cesar Pelli Levi. Iberdrola Tower. Bilbao, Spain. 2007. Street view and floor plan.
Photo credit: anonymous

6.3.19. Cesar Pelli Levi. Petronas Twin Towers. Kuala Lumpur, Malaysia. 1997.
Photo credit: ourplanetimages.com

6.3.20. Mario Botta and Snøhetta. SFMOMA. San Francisco, USA. 1995.
Photo by author

Ginzburg, Louis I. Kahn, Marcel Breuer, Percival Goodman, Bertrand Goldberg, César Pelli Levi, Denise Scott Brown (née Lakofski), and Richard George Rogers made substantial contributions. As already noted, Jewish architects, who had then for the first time entered the profession, brought to it an architecture specifically Jewish in origin.

Daniel Libeskind, a popular Jewish architect of the 21st century, once remarked: "Jews were long deprived of their architectural tradition. We weren't allowed in the profession. I represent only the third generation of Jewish architects. There were none before the twentieth century. And, of course, certain traits of Jewish culture, of the Jewish perception of space, I express in my architecture."[13] Daniel Libeskind has spoken about his Jewishness in architecture in several interviews, as it is a central aspect of his design philosophy. This echoed the earlier statement by Paul Goldberger: "…we can surely say there is a certain Jewish attitude toward the world, and the question naturally arises as to whether this attitude can translate into archi-

---

13   One notable interview where he discussed this topic was with the Jewish Chronicle, a British Jewish newspaper, in 2017.

tecture: a certain skepticism; a constant willingness to ask questions; a belief in justice, fairness, decency and human possibility; a belief in community; and, most of all, a belief that we are not just here to suffer while we await a better world, but to make this world better, right now and right here." [14]

As we have seen, Stanley Tigerman has called Postmodernism a Jewish movement, and Charles Jencks, similarly described Deconstructivism as the brainchild of Jewish architects. He also said that a Jewish sense of the world had a great deal to do with its creation. In his 1991 book The New Paradigm in Architecture: The Language of Post-Modernism Charles Jencks specifically refers to Peter Eisenman, Frank Gehry, Daniel Libeskind, and Richard Meier as the New York Five, a group of architects who were instrumental in the development of Deconstructivism. Jencks notes that these architects were all of Jewish origin and that their shared background informed their architectural sensibilities, which he describes as "emerging from a collective history of displacement, dispossession, and the search for identity."

In sum, *Jewish Architecture* has been reborn after nearly 2,000 years of hibernation, as one of the many consequences of the emancipation of the Jews and the accompanying scientific–technical revolution. But this is an architecture different from the architecture of people long established in their land. This architecture does not cling to historical tradition and knows no national boundaries. Found worldwide in cities like London, New York, Chicago, Singapore, Dubai, Shanghai, Kuwait, and Seoul *Jewish Architecture* seamlessly integrates into the cultural landscape of Israel. It fits there organically within the culture of the reborn land of the Jews.

---

14 See: Goldberger, Paul. *Is there a Jewish Architecture?* A lecture at the Jewish Center of the Hamptons. August 26, 2011. http://www.paulgoldberger.com/lectures/is-there-a-jewish-architecture/

Summary

This book presents a broader definition of human activity termed *Jewish Architecture*, departing from other delineations that associate it solely with buildings constructed by or for Jews. It regards *Jewish Architecture* as a cultural phenomenon, representing a global architectural approach strongly influenced by Jewish vision, methods, and traditions. This architecture advocates for open plans, rational interior designs, the use of cutting-edge building materials and techniques, simplistic structures devoid of embellishments, contemporary aesthetic values, and a cosmopolitan character.

The book fundamentally examines architecture as the process of developing real estate—the habitat. National architecture emerges as a totality of structures on this nation's territory. However, over almost two millennia, Jews have lived on land belonging to others, without the right to own it, preventing the cultivation of a distinct national architecture. Nevertheless, they have consistently influenced local architectural developments. Starting in the late eighteenth century, with the acquisition of equal civil rights, which coincided with the Industrial Revolution Jews began actively acquiring properties and playing a significant role in real estate development within their host nations. Architecture involves a close collaboration between two key players: the client and the architect.

The Industrial Revolution gave rise to a new class of clients—wealthy Jews. However, due to their essentially cosmopolitan nature, these Jewish clients (essentially the architect's partners) were not constrained by specific local traditions and conditions in their architectural pursuits. This dynamic became instrumental in fostering new trends in architecture.

Across many countries, Jews, who initially served as clients and later also as architects, nurtured the modernist architectural movement of the twentieth century. The book demonstrates that over time, the Jewish diaspora emerged as a leading force in shaping modernist architecture, supplanting the art-inspired historicism of previous eras. This architecture embodies a Jewish spirit characterized by dynamism, entrepreneurship, and cosmopolitan flair. In the twentieth century, the entire world experienced a wave of globalization in culture and economy, with the Jewish diaspora playing a significant role in this process. Furthermore, globalization inherently carried elements of the economic ties and cultural cosmopolitanism derived from the Jewish diaspora.

The study presented in this book unveils a significant correlation between globalization and the pivotal role played by the Jewish diaspora in shaping and advancing modern architecture, especially during its formative years. The genesis of this architectural movement can be traced back to Jewish clients who initially conceived it as an innovative typology. Over time, they further nurtured it by assuming the role of patrons, supporting novel architectural endeavors, and eventually evolving into architects themselves. Consequently, this study posits that modern global architecture warrants recognition as Jewish Architecture.

However, like any historical phenomenon, the current era of globalism is not permanent. If humanity is to secure a future on this planet, new developments are inevitable. There are indications that the pendulum may be swinging towards a resurgence of new forms of nationalism, and if this trend persists, new national architectures will emerge. The existing global Jewish Architecture could potentially serve as a foundation for their evolution. With the re-establishment of the State of Israel in the latter half of the twentieth century, Jews gained an opportunity to create their national architecture on their land.

Presently, as the world appreciates the achievements of global Jewish Architecture, national Israeli architecture is beginning to take shape in Israel. However, this architecture does not derive from attempts to stylistically adapt Middle Eastern vernacular architecture; rather, it stems from a major shift in the understanding and definition of architecture that occurred from the late nineteenth century onward. In the future, as globalism may diminish, potentially making way for nationalism, Israel, like other nations, will develop its national architecture based on local conditions, Israeli culture, and traditions. Residential architecture will likely be at the forefront of this development. We can already observe its early stages in the works of leading Israeli architects, such as in the residential developments of

Moshe Safdie in Israeli Modi'in. However, it will not be *Jewish Architecture* but *Israeli Architecture*, grounded in the current global Jewish Architecture.

Bibliography

Abramson, Glenda, ed. Encyclopedia of Modern Jewish Culture. New York: Routledge, 2005. ISBN: 041529813X

Bedoire, Fredric. Ett judiskt Europa – Kring uppkomsten av en modern arkitektur 1830–1930, Carlssons, Stockholm, 1998, (Swedish). English edition: The Jewish Contribution to Modern Architecture 1830–1930, Ktav Publishing House, Jersey City, 2004. ISBN-13: 9780881258080

Berkovich, Gary. Reclaiming a History. Jewish Architects in Imperial Russia and the USSR. Grunberg Verlag. Weimar und Rostock, Germany 2021-2022. IBSN: Vol. 1, 9783933713612; Vol. 2, 9783933713613; Vol. 3, 9783933713643; Vol. 4, 9783933713650

Boman, Thorleif. Hebrew Thought Compared with Greek. W.W. Norton & Company, 1975. ISBN: 9780393005349

Braiterman, Zachary. The Shape of Revelation: Aesthetics and Modern Jewish Thought. Stanford University Press, 2007. ISBN: 9780804753210

Chicago Architecture and Design, 1872-1993. Prestel, NY,1993, ISBN: 3791323458

Choisy, Auguste. Histoire de l'architecture. Tome 1. Paris. Gauthier-Villars, Imprimeur-Libraire. 1899

Cohen, Nahoum. Bauhaus Tel Aviv. B T Batsford, London, 2003. ISBN: 0713487925

Dellheim, Charles. Belonging and Betrayal. How Jews Made the Art World Modern. Brandeis University Press, MA. 2021. ISBN: 9781684580569

Fine, Steven. Writing a history of Jewish Architecture;
https://www.khanacademy.org/humanities/ap-art-history/introduction-cultures-religions-apah/judaism-apah/a/writing-a-history-of-jewish-architecture

Frampton, Kenneth, Modern Architecture – A Critical History. Thames & Hudson, London, 1982

Giedion, Siegfried. Neues Bauen

in Frankreich. Essen und Eisenbeton, Leipzig–Berlin, 1927

Giedion, Siegfried. Space, Time and Architecture. The Growth of a New Tradition. (The Charles Eliot Norton Lectures for 1938–1939), published by Harvard University Press, Cambridge, MA, 1942

Ginzburg, Moisei. Style and Epoch. The MIT Press, 1983. ISBN: 9780262070881

Goldberger, Paul. Is there a Jewish Architecture? A lecture at the Jewish Center of the Hamptons. 08,26,2011. http://www.paulgoldberger.com/lectures/is-there-a-jewish-architecture/

Gruber, Samuel D. American Synagogues. New York, NY. Rizzoli, 2003. ISBN: 0847825493

Gruber, Samuel D., Angeli Sachs, and Edward van Voolen, ed. Jewish Identity in Contemporary Architecture/ Jüdische Identität in Der Zeitgenössischen Architektur. New York: Prestel, 2004. ISBN: 9783791330570

Guyer, Paul. A Philosopher Looks at Architecture. Cambridge University Press. ISBN: 9781108820424

Harries, Karsten. The Ethical Function of Architecture. The MIT Press, 1997. ISBN: 9780262082525

Jacobs, Joseph. Jewish contribution to civilization: an estimate. The Jewish Publication Society of America. Philadelphia. 1919

Jencks, Charles. The New Paradigm in Architecture: The Language of Post-Modernism. Yale University Press, 2002. ISBN: 9780300095135

Jew Age, http://www.jewage.org

Jewish Virtual Library, http://www.jewishvirtuallibrary.org/jsource/judaica/ejud_0002_0002_0_01259.html

Johnson, Paul. A History of the Jews. Harper Perennial, 1988. ISBN-13: 9780060915339

Katz, Jacob. "Baron Adolf von Kniggs: Uber Den Umgang mit Menschen," in Out of the Ghetto: The Social Background of Jewish Emancipation, 1770-1870. Syracuse University Press, 1998. ISBN: 673647750

Kilcher, Andrea, Gabriela Safran, ed. Writing Jewish Culture: Paradoxes in Ethnography. Indiana University Press, 2016. 2. ISBN: 9780253019585

Klein, Rudolf. Architectural modernism: a precursor of cultural globalization. 2022, SmartArt Conference Proceedings; https://www.academia.edu/88325720/

Klein, Rudolf. Jewish Architecture' of the late twentieth century. IZGRADNJA 66, 2012

Klein, Rudolf. Synagogues in Hungary 1782–1918 Genealogy, Typology and Architectural Significance. Budapest: Terc Ltd., 2017. ISBN: 9786155445088

Kravtsov, Sergey R. "The Progressive Synagogue in Lemberg/Lwów/Lviv: Architecture and Community" Academia.edu. 2013. https://www.academia.edu/4536750/_The_Progressive_Synagogue_in_Lemberg_Lwów_Lviv_Architecture_and_Community_?email_work_card=view-paper

Kravtsov, Sergey R. "Jewish Identities in Synagogue Architecture of Galicia and Bukovina" The Bar-Ilan Journal of Jewish Art, 6 (2010), 81–100; https://www.academia.edu/471035/_Jewish_Identities_in_Synagogue_Architecture_of_Galicia_and_Bukovina_

Krinsky, Carol Herselle. Synagogues of Europe: Architecture, History, Meaning. The MIT Press, Cambridge, MA. 1985. ISBN: 0262110970

Kundera, Milan. Abduction of the West or The Tragedy of Central Europe (Unos západu aneb Tragédie střední Evropy). Zagreb: Gordogan, 1985

Loos, Adolf, Die Emanzipation des Judentums. In: Die Schriften 1897–1900, ed. A. Opel, Wien, 1997

Loos, Adolf. On Architecture. Ariadne Press. 2007. ISBN: 9781572410985

Lynn, Richard. The Chosen People: A Study of Jewish Intelligence and Achievement. Whitefish, MT: Washington Summit Publishers, 2011. ISBN: 9781593680367

Muller, Jerry Z. Capitalism and the Jews. Princeton University Press, 2011. ISBN: 978-0691153063

Rosenfeld, Gabriel David. Building After Auschwitz: Jewish Architecture and the Memory of the Holocaust. Yale University Press, November 29, 2011. ISBN: 978-0300169140.

Sachar, Howard M. A History of the Jews in the Modern World. Alfred A. Knoff. 2005. ISBN: 0375414975

Silber, Dr. Mendel. "Jewish Architects" in Jewish Achievement. Saint Louis: Press of "The Modern view", 5670 (1910), pp.41-45 http://www.archive.org/stream/jewishachieveme00silbgoog#page/n15/mode/2up

Skarf, Joshua. ArchitecTorah: Architectural Ideas in Judaism and the Weekly Torah Portion. Urim Publications, 2023. ISBN: 978-965-524-368-0

Slezkine, Yuri. The Jewish Century. Princeton University Press, Princeton and Oxford, 2006. ISBN: 0691119953

Sombart, Werner. The Jews and Modern Capitalism (Die Juden und das Wirtschaftsleben). Leipzig: Duncker und Humblot, 1911

Tietz, Jürgen. The Story of Architecture of the twentieth Century. Könemann, 1999. ISBN: 3829020457

Tigerman, Stanley. Versus. New York: Rizzoli International Publications, Inc., 1982. ISBN: 0847804291

Vitruvius. On Architecture. Harvard University Press. 1914.

Index

Symbols

17th century 33, 48, 78, 80, 83
18th century 13, 73, 80, 170, 175
19th century 15, 33, 80, 88, 90, 163, 164, 167, 169, 170, 177
19th-century 163, 168
20th century 22, 33, 34, 48, 90, 163, 164, 171, 172, 176, 177, 184

A

Adler, Dankmar 145, 164
Afghanistan 54
Albers, Anni 131
Alberti, Leon Battista 35
Aleppo 85, 89
Alighieri, Dante 34
Allen, Woody 158
Altman, Natan 128, 129
Amichai, Yehuda 158
Ancient Greece 60, 61
Ancient Israel 69
Ancient Rome 60, 61, 174
Ando, Tadao 178
Andreu, Paul 184, 187
anti-Semitism 12
Arabian Peninsula 53
architect 14, 16, 17, 18, 35, 37, 41, 165, 168, 172, 176, 178, 184
architecture 13, 14, 15, 16, 17, 18, 21, 22, 29, 30, 33, 34, 35, 37, 38, 41, 42, 43, 44, 46, 47, 48, 50, 53, 54, 56, 58, 59, 60, 61, 62, 64, 65, 66, 67, 69, 70, 71, 72, 73, 74, 75, 76, 77, 78, 80, 83, 85, 88, 90, 163, 164, 165, 167, 168, 169, 170, 171, 172, 173, 174, 175, 176, 177, 178, 184

Architecture 58, 163, 164, 165, 167, 168, 169, 170, 171, 172, 173, 175, 176, 177, 178, 184, 190, 193, 194, 195
ARCHITECTURE 43, 44, 50, 54, 171
ark 88
Art Deco 177
Art Nouveau 163, 176, 177
Astuce, Gabriel 104
Austria 69
Awin, Josef 145

B

Bader, Theodor 96
Baekeland, Leo 94
Baerwald, Alexander 172
Bahrain 56
Bakhman, Leiba 145
Balkans 53
Bamberger, Louis 95
Baroque 35, 167
Barshch, Mikhail 148, 150
Basevi, Elias George 145
Bauhaus 38, 172, 173, 193
Baumhorn, Lipót 145, 164
Beardsley, Aubrey 126
Bedoire, Fredric 95
Bellow, Saul 158
Bengali 50.
Bergson, Henry 184
Berliner, Emil 94
Berlin, Irving 158
Bernini, Giovanni 34, 35
Bernstein, Leonard 158
Bijvoet, Bernard 108, 110
Bila Tserkva 85, 87
Bilbao 22, 41, 184

bimah 83, 88, 169
Bimah 88
Bing, Sigfried 125
Blumenstein, Samuel 94
Bofill, Ricardo 22, 25, 26, 184, 185
Boman, Thorleif 159
Botta, Mario 184, 189
Bramante, Donato 34, 35
Brandt, Marianne 136
Breuer, Marcel 131, 148, 151, 184
Brodsky, Joseph 158
Bronfman, Samuel 108
Brunel, Isambard Kingdom 141
Brunelleschi, Filippo 34, 35
Brunner, Arnold W. 145, 164
Buonarroti, Michelangelo 34, 35

C

Calatrava, Santiago 184, 186
Canterbury 29
Cape Cod house 13, 14
Caucasus 65, 171
Central Asia 48, 54, 71, 171, 177
Central Asian assemblies 14
Cervantes, Miguel de 34
Chagall, Marc 132, 158
Chanel, Coco 131
Chareau, Perré 108
Chartres 29
Chashnik, Ilya 128, 129
China 46, 47, 48, 78, 177, 178, 184
Churchill, Winston 12
Cinquecento 35
Cohen, Nahoum 173
Cone, Etta and Claribel 132
Constructivism 177
Copernicus, Nicolaus 34
Costwold 62
Cubit, Thomas 141

D

Dalbet, Louis 108
Dalsace, Annie and Jean 108

Daniel Libeskind 190
da Vignola, Giacomo Barozzi 35
da Vinci, Leonardo 34
Delaunay, Sonia 129
Dellheim, Charles 132
de Medici, Lorenzo 35
Derrida, Jacques 184
diaspora 11
Disraeli, Benjamin 145
Dymshits-Tolstaya, Sofia 147

E

Egypt 12, 58, 59, 71, 72
Ehrlich, Paul 94
Eiffel, Gustav 141
Eiffel Tower 33, 141, 144
Einstein, Albert 184
Eisenman, Peter 38
Eisenshtat, Sidney 178
England 14, 62, 75
epoch 14, 16, 21, 34
Epstein Palace 101
Ernst, Max 158
Erté 131

F

Fallingwater 108, 117
fashion 21
Fernbach, Henry 145
Fine, Steven 173, 193
Fleischman, Adolph 145
Florence Cathedral 34
Forman, Milos 158
Foster, Norman 178, 183
Fould, Louis 99
France 18, 165, 178, 184
Frankel, Wilhelm 104
Fuerst, Julius 95
Function 16, 21
fusuma 46

200

G

Gabo, Naum 158
Galerie Bernheim 108
Galerie Paul Rosenberg 108
Galeries Lafayette 96, 98
Galilei, Galileo 34
Gallé, Émile 126
Gassho-zukuri farmhouses 45
Gaudí, Antoni 126
Gehry, Frank 22, 24, 38, 39, 108, 121, 148, 155, 165
George, Waldemar 132
Germany 61, 69, 74, 80, 164, 165, 172, 173
Gershwin, George 158
Ginzburg, Moisei 14, 56, 148, 150, 184
Goldberger, Paul 169, 172
Goldman & Salatsch Building 104, 105
Goldschmidt, Leopold 95
Goodman, Percival 178, 180, 184
Gothic 14, 29, 30, 34, 41, 77, 163, 167
Gothic epoch 30
Graham, Bruce 119
Grands Magasins du Printemps 96, 98
Graves, Michael 22
Great Synagogue of Aleppo 85
Great Wild Goose Pagoda 47
Guggenheim Museum 22
Guggenheim, Peggy 132
Guimard, Hector 123
Gumpel, Ludwig 94

H

habitat 13
Hadid, Zaha 38, 40, 178, 185
Hertz, Henrietta 94
Hilberseimer, Ludwig 148, 152
Hilbert, David 94
Hirsch, Hermann 94
Hirsch, Isidor 95
Hirsch, Max 94
Hirsch von, Leopold 95
Hitzig, Georg Friedrich Heinrich 145

Hoffmann, Josef 134, 140
Holocaust 12
Horyuji Temple 46

I

India 42, 48, 50, 80, 177
Industrial Revolution 163, 176, 177
Insull, Samuel 94
Iran 53, 55
Islam 53, 169
Islamic 30, 33, 50, 53, 54, 77, 168

J

Jacobs, Joseph 12, 123, 156, 160
Jaluzot, Jules 96
Japan 42, 44, 78, 177
Jesus Christ 184
Jewish 11, 12, 13, 16, 21, 41, 43, 44, 67, 69, 70, 71, 72, 73, 74, 75, 76, 78, 80, 83, 85, 88, 90, 163, 164, 165, 167, 168, 169, 170, 171, 172, 173, 174, 175, 176, 177, 178, 184
Jewish architects 163, 165, 167, 168, 170, 172, 174, 178, 184
Jewish Architecture 13, 16, 21, 71, 76, 88, 163, 165, 170, 171, 174, 175, 176, 177, 178
Jewish Century 177, 195
Jewish Identity 21, 67
Jewish nation 11, 12
Jewish style 21, 41
Jews 11, 12, 13, 70, 71, 74, 77, 78, 80, 85, 88, 90, 164, 167, 169, 171, 173, 174, 175, 176, 177, 178, 184
John Hancock Center 108
Judaism 11, 168, 169, 170

K

Kafka, Franz 158
Kahn, Alphonse 96
Kaifeng Jews 78, 171
Kandinsky, Wassily 131

Katherine Dock Warehouses 141
Kerala 50, 80
Kfar Nakhum Synagogue 175
Khidekel', Lazar 128, 129
Kings Cross Station 141, 143
Kleinerman, Zalman 145
Klein, Rudolf 161, 172, 184
Klimt, Gustav 123, 126.
Kohn, Aron Hirsch 94
Kohn, Aron Hirsch 94
Koolhaas, Rem 178
Korn, Arthur 148, 151
Kotlyar, E. 85
Krasner, Jonathan B 13
Kravtsov, Sergey R 171
Krinsky, Carol Herselle 77
Kubrick, Stanley 158
Kundera, Milan 157
Kurzweil, Max 123
Kuwait 56, 190

L

Labrouste, Henri 99
Lalique, René 126
Lamm, Carl Robert 99
Lauterbach, Edward 94
Lazama Synagogue 88, 89
Lazard, Samuel 94
Le Corbusier 18, 20, 99, 108, 114, 115
Lempicka de, Tamara 131
Leopold Eidlitz 164
Levinas, Emanuel 184
Levi, Primo 158
Levy, Abraham 99
Libeskind, Daniel 38, 148, 155, 184
Ligeti, György 184
Lilien, Ephraim Moses 123
Lipchitz, Jacques 132, 158
Lipót Baumhorn 164
Lissitzky, El 128, 129, 130
London 22, 173, 178, 190, 193
Loos, Adolf 16, 99, 104, 105, 106, 107, 176
Ludwig Levy 164, 165

Lurcat, Andre 108, 116
Lynn, Richard 156

M

Machiavelli, Niccolò 34
Mackintosh, Charles Rennie 99, 122, 126, 134, 138
Mackintosh, Margaret Macdonald 122, 124
Mahler, Gustav 158
Maimonides 184
Maison de Verre 108, 110
Majolica House 104, 106
Mandelstam, Osip 158
Marx, Claude-Roger 132
Marx, Karl 184
Meerzon, Iosif 146, 147
Meier, Richard 165, 178, 182
Mendelsohn, Erich 148, 149
Mesopotamia 58
Mexica 66
Michelangelo Buonarroti 35
Michelin family 126
Middle East 53, 71, 85, 177
mikveh 88
Milosz, Czeslaw 158
Minka residences 45
Minkowski, Hermann 94
Mocatta, David 144
Modern 41, 172, 184
Modigliani, Amedeo 132, 158
Moholy-Nagy, László 131
Mond, Ludwig 95
Moore, Charles 22
Moorish Revival 41, 146, 167, 168, 169, 170, 171
More, Thomas 34
Morgenthau, Henry 99
Morocco 55, 73, 88
Moscow 18, 58
Moser, Koloman 123
Mucha, Alphonse 123, 126, 127
Muller, J 93

Murray, Matthew 93
Muslim 50, 53, 54, 56, 72, 74, 167, 168

N

Nadelman, Elie 158
Nagasaki 78
Nasher, Raymond and Patsy 132

Nazis 172
Neutra, Richard 148, 153, 184

Nevelson, Louise 158
Newcomen, Thomas 93
Nobel Prize 13
North Africa 53

O

Olbrich, Joseph Maria 134, 137
Oppenheim, Solomon 94
Oranienburgerstrasse synagogue 99, 100
Oregon 22

P

Paddington Station 141, 142
Palace Europe 97
Palladio, Andrea 35
Paris 25, 26, 95, 96, 97, 98, 104, 108, 109, 110, 116, 122, 123, 125, 132, 135, 144
Pelli Levi, César 184
People of Israel 11
Péreire brothers 93
Perret, Auguste 104
Petrarca, Francesco 34
Pe, I. M. 178, 183
Piano, Renzo 178
Pissarro, Camille 132
Podillia 64
Poiret, Paul 131
Poland 83, 85, 88, 173
Polanski, Roman 158
Poltava 64
Polyakov brothers 93, 99
Popper, Julius 94

Poznański, Julius 94
Prigogine, Ilya 184

Q

Qatar 56

R

Raphael 34, 35
Rathenau, Emil 95
Rechter, Ze'ev 174
Reese, Michael 95
Renaissance 14, 15, 29, 33, 34, 35, 37, 41, 58, 61, 167, 176
Ringstrasse 99
Rodchenko, Aleksandr 129
Rogers, Richard George 184
Rohe van der, Mies 17, 99
Romans 12
Ronchamp 18
Rosenthal, Julius 94
Rosenwald, Julius 95, 99
Rothko, Mark 158
Rothschild de, James 96
Rothschild, Mayer 95
Rothschilds 93
Rubinstein, Helena 132
Ruhlmann, Émile-Jacques 131
Russia 12, 18, 65, 76, 85, 88

S

Safdie, Moshe 148, 154, 192
Salmon, André 132
Sassoon, David 95
Saudi Arabia 55
Savoy, Pierre 104
Schapira, Max 94
sculpture 13, 17, 34, 35, 38, 41
Seagram Building 108

Seder 12
Seligman, Joseph 99
seventeenth century 33
Shakespeare, William 34
Shapiro, Tevel' 146, 147
Shekhtel, Fyodor 102
Siberia 65, 85, 173
Singer, Isaac Bashevis 158
Sinyavskii, Mikhail 148, 150
Slezkine, Yuri 93, 157, 161
Solomon Guggenheim Museum 108
Solvay, Ernest 95
Sombart, Werner 93
Soutine, Chaim 132
Spain 88, 173, 184
Speyer, Jerry 108
Spinoza, Baruch 184
St. Basil's Cathedral 18
Steiner House 104, 106, 107
Steiner, Lilly and Hugo 104
Stein, Gertrude 126, 132
Stein, Michel 99
Stephenson, George 93
Stiassny, Wilhelm 164, 165
Stickley, Gustav 122, 124
Stirling, James 22
Straus, Oscar 95
Strauss, Abraham 95
Strauss, Levi 95
Struck, Hermann 123
Style 14, 16, 21, 169, 170, 177
synagogues 38, 67, 71, 72, 76, 77, 78, 80, 83, 85, 88, 165, 167, 168, 169, 170, 175, 178

T

Talmud 77
Tatlin, Vladimir 129, 147, 148
Taut, Bruno 148, 152
Telford, Thomas 141
Tempietto in Rome 34
Temple of Heaven 48
Théâtre des Champs-Élysées 104, 109

Tiergarten 99, 100
Tiffany, Louis Comfort 126
Tigerman, Stanley 22, 159
timber-framed walls 61
Tishman, Robert 108
Todaiji Temple 46
Todesco Palace 101
Tomsk 65, 85, 86
Torah 12
Toulouse-Lautrec de, Henri 123, 126
Tudor 62
Tugendhat family 99
Tugendhat, Grete and Fritz 108
Tunis 73

U

Ukraine 64, 85
Ukrainian 75, 167
Ullman, Leopold 94

V

Vauxcelles, Louis (Louis Meyer) 132
Veblen, Oswald 94
Villa Guggenbuhl 108, 116
Villa Meyer 108, 114
Villa Perl 114
Villa Savoye 104, 109
Villa Stein 108, 115
Vitruvius, Marcus 16

W

Warchavchik, Gregori 148, 153
Warndorfer, Fritz 99, 126, 132
Windcatchers 55
Wittgenstein, Karl 94, 99, 126
Wittgenstein, Ludwig Josef Johann 99
Wolman, Jerry 108
Wright, Frank Lloyd 16, 17, 108, 117, 118

Y

Yamasaki, Minoru 178, 179
Yemen 55
Yorkshire 62

Z

Zevi, Bruno 176
Zolochiv Synagogue 85
Zuckerkandl, Victor 134

Illustration Credits

Every possible effort has been made to acknowledge the ownership of copyright images included in this book, as indicated in picture captions. Errors, if any, will be corrected in subsequent editions, if the publisher is notified.

Berkovich, Gary
Jewish Architecture

Copyright © 2024 by Gary Berkovich
All rights reserved

No part of this book may be reproduced in any form or by any means, electronic, mechanical, photocopying, or otherwise, without the prior written permission of the author, except for the use of brief quotations in a book review.

Book interior and cover design by Gary Berkovich

ISBN 978-1-68082-056-0
Published in the United States by ALMAZ
10 9 8 7 6 5 4 3 2 1
First Edition

www.ingramcontent.com/pod-product-compliance
Lightning Source LLC
Chambersburg PA
CBHW041610220426
43668CB00001B/2